Paul Harris

How to sight-read

The art and science behind developing sight-reading technique

> *A companion to the **Improve your sight-reading!** series revealing sight-reading as a technique that can be both taught and learnt by all who wish to develop it.*

© 2023 by Paul Harris
First published in 2023 by Faber Music Ltd
Brownlow Yard, 12 Roger Street, London WC1N 2JU
Music processed by Donald Thomson
Text and cover design by Elizabeth Ogden
Printed in England by Caligraving Ltd
All rights reserved

ISBN10: 0-571-54307-3
EAN13: 978-0-571-54307-6

To buy Faber Music publications or to find out about the full range of titles available please contact your local music retailer or Faber Music sales enquiries:

Faber Music Ltd, Burnt Mill, Elizabeth Way, Harlow CM20 2HX
Tel: +44 (0) 1279 82 89 82
fabermusic.com

Contents

Foreword   5
The aim of this book   8

Part 1 Setting the scene
- 1.1 Everyone can sight-read!   10
- 1.2 Demystifying sight-reading   16
- 1.3 What will make a better sight-reader?   21

Part 2 Aspects of knowledge
- 2.1 The process of reading   24
- 2.2 Introducing pulse, rhythm and pitch   27
- 2.3 Why is all this important and what some are seeing   31

Part 3 Developing sight-reading technique
- 3.1 Knowledge and deepening understanding of ingredients   34
- 3.2 Hearing it in our heads   36
- 3.3 Brain processing speed and pattern recognition   37
- 3.4 Peripheral vision and looking ahead   40
- 3.5 Walking the course   42
- 3.6 Key awareness   46
- 3.7 Subdivision   49
- 3.8 Location awareness and fingering   54
- 3.9 Improvisation   57
- 3.10 Piano-specific techniques   60

Part 4 Practical matters
- 4.1 Teaching and practising sight-reading   63
- 4.2 Sight-reading in exams   70
- 4.3 The first encounter with notation   74
- 4.4 FAQs   76

Final thought   78

Foreword

The ability to sight-read is an essential skill for any musician, but something that is too often neglected as part of the pedagogical process. The reasons for this can stem from perceptions that as a skill it cannot be taught, that it will evolve organically as part of the learning process, or that it is something that the student simply can or cannot do. Paul Harris' book dispels these myths by providing a systematic approach for both tutor and student that conceptualises sight-reading as being at the heart of the overall learning process – an accessible skill that everyone can acquire and develop with confidence.

Whether it is about learning new repertoire quickly and efficiently or playing or singing in an ensemble context, it is clear that being able to sight-read accurately and fluently with an appreciation of style and interpretation brings significant advantages. The first time a student plays any new repertoire at any level can be critical to the final outcome, as mis-readings in the initial learning process are generally more complex and time consuming to address retrospectively. When playing in an ensemble, this can be especially frustrating for others, whose experience is inevitably compromised by the time taken for everyone to reach the same stage in the rehearsal process.

Historically the compartmentalised nature of music examinations has arguably reinforced the stereotype of sight-reading as an 'added extra': a separate detached component that carries a proportionately smaller number of marks to the pieces, so tends to have a negligible impact on the overall result. Unfortunately, this embeds the view that being able to sight-read is an option rather than it being central to the holistic process of developing into a skilled and rounded musician. This is a central theme of this book, which emphasises the importance of being able to sight-read and seeks to encourage all teachers and students to adopt a more practical and engaging approach.

Quality pedagogy is of course founded on supporting the individual to fulfil their potential and musical aspirations through a personalised approach. This recognises different starting points, challenges and end goals, all of which need to be addressed in a bespoke and individualised way. On this basis, Paul's book should be viewed as an essential source of advice and guidance to complement other resources and something that can be adapted and customised as appropriate to meet the needs of the individual learner. As such, it is a valuable and timely addition to the existing literature, presented in an highly engaging and accessible way.

Professor Linda Merrick CBE
Principal, Royal Northern College of Music

For years, sight-reading has been a neglected area of music education. There is never enough time in half-an-hour's lesson to do everything, is there? Sight-reading should not only be considered important, it should be *integral*. The advantages of quick reading are huge, enabling players to learn repertoire more quickly and aiding musical and brain development. An orchestra or band will never wait for you when reading for the first time.

Paul Harris has offered the concept that sight-reading is simply a technique that can be easily learnt by us all. He has shown that it is indeed a skill that can be improved and developed. He covers each ingredient thoroughly and offers helpful solutions. *How to sight-read* is an in-depth guide to help improve this most important of skills, develop it as a technique and deepen your understanding of it. This is a must-read for music students and teachers.

John Hutchins
Director Junior Academy and LRAM course, Royal Academy of Music

In this brilliantly conceived guide, Paul Harris demystifies sight-reading in such a clear and direct way, easily accessible to children and adults alike. As he explains, sight-reading is simply a skill to be acquired, one that opens so many doors and brings with it so much enjoyment. This skill is acquired through focused practice – the app allowing that practice to be tailored to the individual's current level of expertise, building confidence securely and musically.

Rooted in a sophisticated understanding of how the brain processes new information and builds knowledge, Paul Harris's approach to musical learning is one that nurtures innate musicianship and encourages increasing levels of skill and sophistication. This is a world away from the 'school of correction' that is still seen in some parts of formal music education today. Above all, he shows how learning is consistently rewarding and sight-reading can be enormous fun!

Simon Toyne
Executive Director of Music, David Ross Education Trust and President, Music Teacher's Association

This positive, pleasurable and innovative approach to developing reading skills has a distinctly holistic methodology. It features, amongst many areas, the gradual development of reflexes, recall, peripheral vision and awareness of rhythmic subdivision. The book also stresses the great importance of scales and musical patterns if one wants to succeed. The accompanying sight-reading app will be fun for all to use, providing a pathway for this multi-faceted methodology to be practised with an enjoyable sense of progress and fulfilment.

Murray McLachlan
Head of Keyboard, Chetham's School of Music; Artistic Director,
Chetham's International Summer School; international concert pianist

The aim of this book

… is simply to encourage and show how anyone (and everyone) can become a more effective and proficient musician through the ability to sight-read with confidence.

Sight-reading and reading

The ability to read music is simply just that – an ability to read musical notation and know, fairly instantly and fairly accurately, *what it means*. Just like you're reading these words. More specifically, reading music implies knowing what it sounds like, knowing how to bring it to life (accurately) on your instrument or voice and doing so with musical expression. The term 'sight-reading' is just doing it, in relation to some particular notation, for the first time. After that, we are *re-reading* that same material. But that's not a term we normally use, or for which we really have any need.

Often the terms *reading* and *sight-reading* are used a little arbitrarily. Where necessary, and if appropriate, I shall try to make a distinction between them.

Who the book is for

This book is aimed at all who wish to develop their sight-reading skills. It is for all instrumental and singing teachers, in all genres, who would like to incorporate the teaching of sight-reading regularly into their work. It is for students at virtually any point in their musical development once they are past the elementary levels of learning, and it will also be helpful to parents who may like to gain an understanding and insight of this fundamental but so often misunderstood and neglected element of musical development.

On occasion I have aimed to make a difference in the expectations and examples between beginner and more advanced sight-readers. But in the main I have tried to concentrate on, describe, and explain what I believe to be a set of comprehensive principles that will apply to *all* levels.

The sight-reading web app

There are three particular areas of sight-reading technique that I thought would benefit from the kind of activities a web app can generate. I have been working for many months with John Williams who has developed the programme to do exactly what I had hoped for. We have 'road-tested' it extensively and responded to many interesting comments, and I hope you will find it both fun and helpful. You will discover more about it and how to use it as the three areas appear later on. Access the web app by going to paulharristeaching.co.uk/sight-reading-app or by scanning the QR code.

The survey

As part of my research in preparing this book I carried out a survey which attracted approximately 150 respondents, made up mostly of players and teachers, but also a number of students of varying ages. I asked a number of questions relating to the way teachers and students approached sight-reading and their attitudes towards it. I have drawn on their responses and these are often quoted and discussed in the text.

Thanks

As always, I have many to thank who have helped in putting this book together. I have been discussing many of the scientific aspects with specialist optometrist, Debra Grant BSc (Hons) MCOptom, ophthalmic optician Karen Lamb, and with a group of friends and musicians who have a particular interest in the subject: Sally Adams, Kate Bowers, Vanessa Bowers, Jean Cockburn, Pat Hayler, Georgina Lee, Dr Maria Luca, Katya Ness, Peter Smalley and students from the Northamptonshire Music and Performing Arts Trust, Dr Caroline Tjoa, Harriet Wells, and Jonathan Whiting. And, of course, the whole project would not have been possible without my wonderful team at Faber Music, especially Emily Bevington and Lesley Rutherford.

1 Setting the scene

1.1 Everyone can sight-read!

They really can!

If someone really aspires to perfect the art of sight-reading, and they are taught, or they learn, in a logical, sequential and systematic way, there is nothing that should prevent them from achieving this aim entirely comprehensively. And let's dispel a belief I've heard time and time again: *sight-reading is one of the most difficult things a musician has to do.* No! Sight-reading is not difficult! Or, to be more precise, it's not *inherently* difficult if approached in the right way. This book presents sight-reading as a technique that, like the *technique* of playing an instrument or singing, can be acquired by recognising and working through a series of carefully ordered and connected activities that bring together and combine, and then develop a particular skill set. A skill set that adds up to being able to sight-read confidently, fluently and accurately.

Some statistics and comments from the survey

Before I began writing, I carried out a sight-reading survey that attracted around 150 responses. Here is some interesting background information gathered from those responses:

- 40% of teachers said they haven't always been able to sight-read.
- 85% of teachers said they enjoy sight-reading.
- 50% of pupils, according to their teachers, do not enjoy sight-reading. Whereas, interestingly, a significantly higher proportion (80%) of students responded saying they *do* enjoy their sight-reading!

I also asked why those students either *like* sight-reading and/or find it challenging. There were a number of representative responses that I kept in mind as I was writing:

- *It creates stress, especially in exams*
- *I can't process the music quickly enough*
- *I make mistakes and that makes me frustrated*
- *I like the challenge of playing something that you've not seen before – there's less pressure to be perfect*
- *I can't deal with the time pressure*
- *I find practising sight-reading boring and unfulfilling*
- *I find melody okay but rhythm complicated*

- *I'm quite good at it, so I enjoy the success*
- *There's too much to understand*
- *I find quick-thinking stressful*
- *I find reading two lines at a time challenging*
- *I like to stop and correct mistakes so it's never fluent*
- *Being able to play something fairly instantly is really satisfying*
- *I can't remember to include all the ingredients at the same time*
- *I hate getting it wrong*

All these issues (and their resolutions) are considered in this book.

The sight-reading myth

There has been a myth among musicians of all kinds, seemingly held since time immemorial, that *some can sight-read and some cannot*. Like some magical quality that some possess and others do not… and the belief is that sight-reading is not really something that can be taught.

There are reasons for this:

Many teachers simply don't teach it. Such teachers probably belong to the group that believe in the *sight-reading myth* and thus assume it is something that can't be taught.

> 'When I was a kid my teacher seemed to think I'd just be able to do it – I was never actually taught.'
>
> 'I was never taught how to do it myself so don't know how to teach it.'

Teachers are experts – experts in teaching and playing their instrument or voice but not experts in sight-reading. So, in general they don't teach it. One teacher summed it up well: *'If it can be taught, better to leave it to someone else who is an expert in that field.'*

Many teachers (if they are good at sight-reading) are probably **instinctive** *sight-readers themselves,* who, for some reason, have always been able to do it and so also happily subscribe to the myth. They, almost certainly, weren't taught to sight read by their teachers. Here's a response from one teacher summarising this point rather succinctly:

> 'It can be hard to teach because I don't remember ever finding it difficult myself.'

Teachers don't think there's enough time – there's so much to do in an already overcrowded lesson that giving any of that precious time over to teaching, practising or learning sight-reading is probably not going to happen. Except possibly when there's an exam looming and the not-so-uncommon: *'we'd better do a bit of sight-reading, in a sort of mildly panic-ridden atmosphere, during the last couple of minutes of the lesson'* approach takes place, causing a similarly panic-like approach from the student at the actual exam.

Teachers think most of their students can't do it anyway and so the thought of trying to teach it is simply impractical and really not worth the effort. Another response from the survey:

> 'It's difficult to teach as my students can't do it and I can't understand why!'

Interestingly, in the early days of learning to play an instrument – working through a method book, for example – students are doing quite a lot of reading and if teachers generally try to avoid teaching in the *'this is how it goes'* or *'listen to me play it first'* kind of way, many more students would be able to sight-read a lot more confidently.

There is a sort of divergence at this point, depending to some extent on which instrument you are teaching. I am about to make some broad generalisations here – but nevertheless they hold more than a little weight and credibility:

- Singers usually do very little reading from musical notation (understandably) and usually know the music (and words) already, having heard it and learnt it aurally. So the actual process of tracking their eyes along a notated line of music whilst singing may be quite unfamiliar.
- Pianists often learn (at least to some extent) by rote (which means they are not gaining independence). A reason many give up.
- Players of orchestral instruments, on the whole (though it is another generalisation) are sometimes a little more confident in their approach to reading (though often *a little* is, realistically, the case).

There's yet another important point to mention here: as we learn our spoken language skills, we obviously do a lot of reading. We need to learn something from this. Beginner instrumental tutor books are usually (and understandably) written in a manner where the next 'stage' introduces some new technical, musical or reading feature in a linear and progressive way. Ideally, we should find lots more material to read and play – at *each* stage, before we move on. It would really make quite a difference.

Everyone DOES sight-read

In fact, most of us inevitably do a reasonable amount of sight-reading when we learn a new piece. But if we know the piece by ear or the teacher tells or shows us how it goes then the significance of having to 'sight-read' it is considerably reduced. The truth is we're not really sight-reading at all because most of the reading and understanding has already been taken care of. The notation takes on the role of a kind of *aide-memoire*.[1]

---

[1] Whereby the notation is simply supporting aural and muscle memory.

So, what's the point of sight-reading?

One respondent to my survey wrote:

> *'It is difficult to convey the value of sight-reading to someone who doesn't understand it, enjoy it or won't do it.'*

So, let's spend some lesson time sharing the considerable benefits of sight-reading with our students.

The various reasons have been reiterated many times – often by exam boards, many of whom (appropriately and for very sound educational reasons) include sight-reading as part of their requirements. But it's important to reconsider these reasons and put them in the context of the ever-changing world in which we now live.

... we can learn pieces quicker

If students can read, the learning and assimilation of new material can become surprisingly quick. And so more pieces can be learnt. That is very motivational for students.

... we can play/sing with others

The joy of music-making with fellow players and singers in whatever context cannot be over-emphasised. Joining a group, an ensemble, an orchestra, a choir – whatever – without that fear of *will I be able to read the music and keep up with the others* is inestimable. So many have been put off joining in the first place or have quit groups, having felt their reading skills were not sufficient. We must do our best to ensure that this doesn't happen. Playing music or singing together is an act of harmony and accord – an activity in which we learn to move and work together with a unified positive ambition; a place to which we need to aspire maybe more now than ever before.

... it changes the role of teaching, learning and practice

If our students can read notation confidently, we will spend much less time teaching *how the piece goes*. We can use that valuable time and our valuable talents and experience to work on aspects that are much more interesting and fun… and musical. And students can do the same during their practice.

... we get more marks in exams

Well … obviously. This doesn't really need any further explanation, but when you consider how much simpler the reading level and complexity of a sight-reading piece within an exam context is in comparison to the pieces just played or sung, you really have to ask why sight-reading is so problematic for so many. If the ingredients in the pieces were really understood, the sight-reading should feel very doable. But so often it isn't – and that must tell us something.

And probably the most important reason of all:

Gaining independence, and ultimately guaranteeing the continuation of our great art.

It's simple: if players and singers can't read, then (without a teacher) they will struggle to learn new material, they may become frustrated and they may give up. On the other hand, an all-embracing independence can be successfully achieved for musicians when they are confident, to a significant extent, in their reading and sight-reading skills. And so they will be able to continue making music *independently* with the double advantage of having a wonderful skill for life and knowing that they are contributing to the survival of this great art.

Vocabulary

In discussing the act of reading and sight-reading there are some words about which we need to agree a definition, and subsequently ensure that our students wholly understand them. I hope you'll agree with mine, which are fashioned from the most reliable sources:

Time A word that has multiple meanings in the context of 'life' more generally, but from a musical point of view, *time* is *the number and arrangement of beats in the bar, e.g. simple duple time.*

Time signature is the pair of numbers found at the start of most pieces or songs. It indicates how many (the top number) of a particular note value (the lower number) are contained in each bar. The lower number also indicates how the notes are grouped.

Playing in time usually means maintaining a steady pulse in relation to tempo.

Tempo is an Italian word and actually means 'time', though musically speaking we usually use it to express the speed or pace of the music in question. A slow or fast tempo, for example. It's often measured in beats per minute (bpm) which is also indicated by the numbers found on a metronome.

Pulse is the division of time (time in its non-musical sense) into regular units.

Beat is the name given to each of those units.

Metre is the grouping of beats into patterns of strong and weak. The time signature is central in indicating what the metre might be.

Rhythm is an interesting word! It comes from the Latin word *Rhythmos* which itself comes from the Greek word *rhuthmos* (ῥυθμός) which actually means flow or movement. So, in collaboration with the other words we've described above, let's go with:

Rhythm is a sense of movement defined by a succession of strong and weak elements

That's probably what we mean when we say 'that was a really rhythmical performance'.

On a more practical level, the word rhythm is also used to refer to a succession of notes with particular values of duration – 'let's clap the rhythm of this four-bar phrase', for example. Interestingly the rhythmic value of a note doesn't really tell us 'how long the note is' but more accurately (and musically), when to start the next note (or rest). The actual sounding duration of a note is very much connected to the style and character of the music being played. And for an instrument like the harpsichord, the length of all notes, once sounded, reduce very quickly beyond our control.

1.2 Demystifying sight-reading

Why can't we sight-read?

Let's take the not uncommon 'exam experience' as a starting point. Candidate has played their pieces quite adequately but is dreading the impending sight-reading test. They look at the dizzying notation now on the music stand and all seems to go hazy in their minds.

We need to take a moment out at this point and consider the *triune brain model*.[2]

[2] As formulated by the American neuroscientist Paul MacLean in the 1960s. More recent investigation and research has found that the three 'elements' he labels work more simultaneously and collaboratively than originally thought. But it still remains a very useful and largely accurate way to understand brain activity.

The brain is divided into three areas:

- The neocortex (the cerebrum) – which is the rational brain where our thinking happens
- The limbic system, or the emotional brain
- The reptilian brain (the cerebellum and brain stem) – which is famously fight or flight … or freeze.

When we panic, we tend to go into reptilian brain mode. The blood bypasses both the rational and the emotional brain and it gives us, for self-protection purposes, a binary choice between fighting or fleeing. All our energies are then focussed on one of those two choices which will, hopefully, result in survival. There is a third option when the situation doesn't call for either of the first two 'f's. Under such panic conditions, the brain simply 'freezes' and everything turns to a dizzying mush. I have seen this happen on so many occasions in the exam room.

And, of course, it happens because these musicians haven't usually been taught *how* to develop their sight-reading skills.

A weakness in reading skills outside the exam room is also quite a common problem, leaving the teacher to indicate, in whatever way they usually prefer, how the piece or song goes.

As already mentioned, sight-reading is not a quality some possess and some don't, and in Part 3 we shall learn *how* it can be developed, eliminating any doubt in the mind of any player or singer about whether they *can* actually develop the ability.

Knowing where you are

It's helpful, as you or a student sets out on this journey, to have some basic musical ingredients already installed in the brain – but it's by no means essential. If they are not there it's not a problem, they can of course be learned, systematically, along the way. But this knowledge is ultimately essential in developing really fluent and accurate sight-reading. For those who have maybe already struggled with some of these ingredients, there are methodical and entirely understandable ways in which to learn them.

So, where are you with music theory?
And just before you answer, here's a bold statement:

Theory is okay!

It's so useful to have some basic knowledge tucked away in the long-term memory to draw upon when it's needed. We sometimes call this basic music knowledge 'theory', but it's really just having labels with which to describe musical ingredients. And, as far as sight-reading goes, some basic understanding of those labels.

If you or a particular student happens to have passed a theory exam (or similar) then you should have enough theoretical knowledge (that will include those labels) to begin moving forwards quite quickly. Ultimately it *is* necessary to know about and understand:

- The various note lengths and their labels (crotchets/quarter notes, etc.)
- The pitch names of notes
- Time signatures
- Key signatures
- Other markings (tempo, character, articulation, performance instructions and so on)

But if you or a student don't have this understanding at this time, it doesn't matter. What matters is that gaps are objectively acknowledged and then filled carefully.

Where are you with scales?
Knowing scales (and therefore key signatures) is certainly useful. More so if they have been learned from notation rather than just from memory. Scales are so useful for developing technique, muscle memory and beyond that, for a whole host of other musically related benefits – and they needn't be boring or dreary to learn.[3]

Do you play computer games?
Some computer games (not all) demand quick reactions and therefore develop quick brain-processing speeds. We shall look at this kind of development as a core skill in building sight-reading technique later. But for now, playing computer games can have a positive and educationally productive side!

[3] I have created a fun method for learning scales in my *Improve Your Scales!* series (Faber Music); there are versions from beginner level for most instruments.

The four pillars of language

Language has, basically, four aspects:

- we speak it,
- we hear it,
- we write it,
- and we read it.

Our language (let's call this form of language, *human language*) allows us to communicate in many different and often subtle ways. Music is also a language; through it we also communicate, and it too has four aspects – each representing a musical version of human language:

- **Playing or singing** is the musical equivalent of **speaking.**
  That's what most of us can do happily and to whatever level we wish.

- **Aural** aspects are the musical equivalent of **hearing.**
  We can hear music on many different levels: simply listening to it and enjoying the sonic experience; hearing it and being affected on an emotional level or hearing it more analytically with awareness of structure, harmony, texture, instrumentation or style, for example. The expression 'aural' also includes hearing, processing and understanding music *internally* using our 'inner ear'.

- **Music notation** (a subset under the general heading of theory) is the equivalent of **writing.**
  Writing music requires a knowledge of basic theory and the various necessary rules and conventions.

- **Reading** is **reading!**
  And when we read a piece of music for the first time, it is known as sight-reading. *Which is what this book is all about.*

Of course, none of this will be any kind of revelation, but thinking along these lines can be very useful as we embark on the journey to sight-reading music with the same confidence and speed we have when reading these words.

Simultaneous Learning and the pillars

[4] If not, you may like to read *Simultaneous Learning*, (Faber Music).

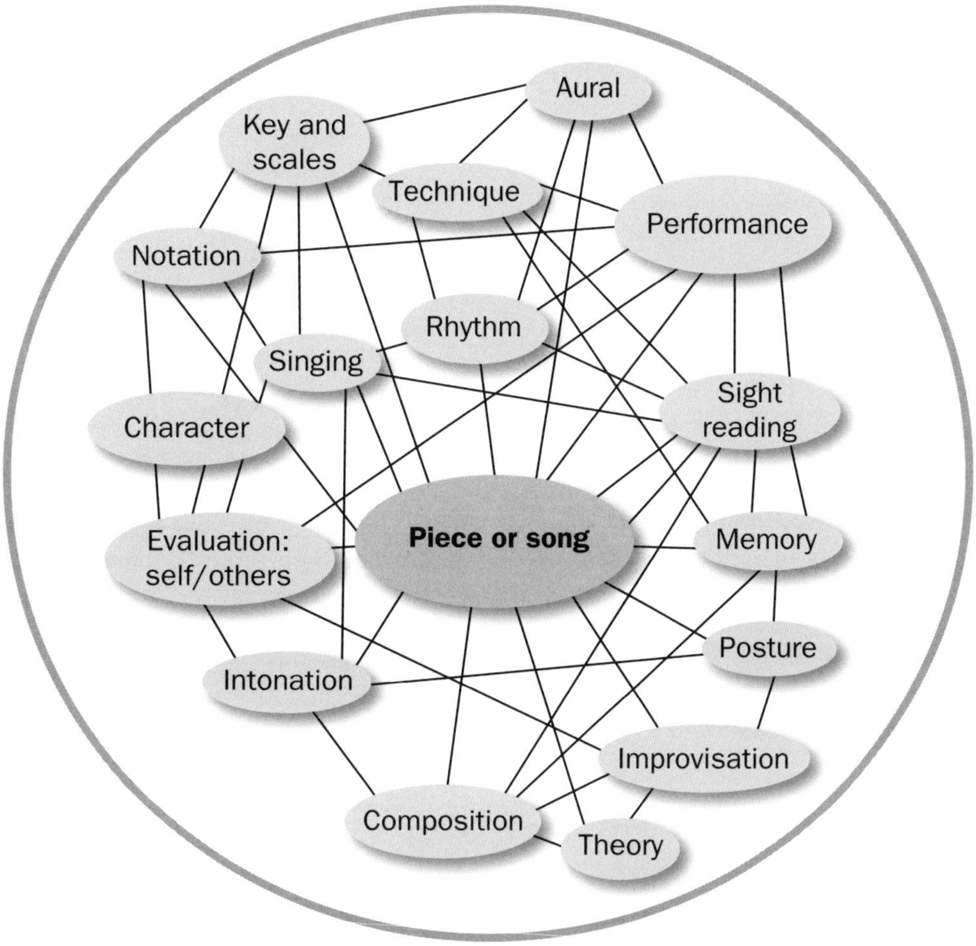

You may be familiar with my concept of Simultaneous Learning[4] – a holistic (and caring) approach to learning and teaching music that leads to real understanding. One of the three main principles is that all the areas of music ultimately connect, which is represented in my Simultaneous Learning Musical Map of the World:

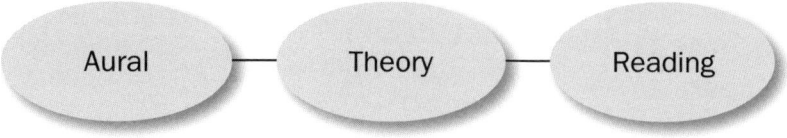

Whilst virtually all the areas in our musical world connect with playing or singing (the first of our four pillars of language), it's the other three pillars that are most pertinent to this book:

Aural — Theory — Reading

Now let's define them:

- **Aural** is about processing and understanding the ingredients of music by ear (be it through our outward hearing or our inner ear).

- **Theory** is about processing, understanding *and describing* the ingredients of music – which may be by ear or through what we see.

- **Reading** is about processing and understanding music we see (the notation).[5]

[5] Sight-reading is the term we use for reading a particular piece for the first time.

They are then, more or less, the same thing – or at least represent the same thing seen from slightly different angles. Maybe we can represent them as three sides of a triangle:

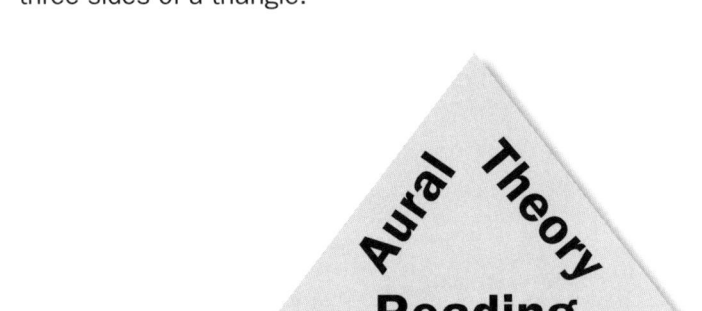

These three pillars of musical language are indeed strongly interconnected, and we will find that understanding their strong connection will contribute to the development of a powerful sense of musicianship. Aural and theory will be constant companions on our journey to develop the technique of sight-reading and being able to do so fluently, accurately and musically.

1.3 What will make a better sight-reader?

There are three areas for exploration on the journey to mastering sight-reading:

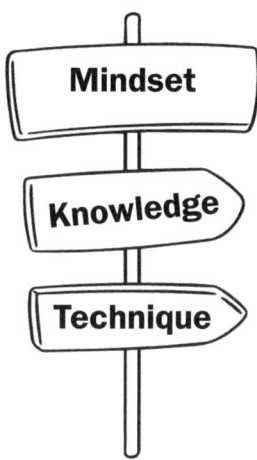

Let's look at each in turn and how they interact to form the basis of learning in order to improve sight-reading skills.

Mindset: how we feel about it

This has to come first, because without a positive attitude towards sight-reading you're not going to get very far with any of the other aspects!

Once it is realised that sight-reading is a technique that anyone can learn and develop by approaching it in logical and sequential incremental stages – just like instrumental or singing technique – then the learner will grow in confidence[6], knowing that it is a journey that will result in a very well-defined, noticeable and measurable improvement.

An optimistic and confident attitude is further enhanced by always remembering to think and use language positively. Never, 'I didn't do that very well', or 'that wasn't very good', but rather, 'how could I have done that better?' or 'What could I do differently next time to create a different and better outcome?' Not, 'I should be able to do that,' and then get frustrated, but instead, 'I'll try that again, but this time…'.

Continuous negativity is toxic – it can build up to a point where we simply give up. If you, or a student, seem to be guilty of taking the more negative approach, aim to break the cycle and begin to develop a more positive approach. If something seems too difficult then it's probably the wrong thing to be doing at that time. Always remember the importance of doing the right thing in the right order and for the right reasons – then nothing will be too difficult.

[6] When we are confident and happy with what we are doing, the body releases hormones like serotonin, glutamate and dopamine. These contribute to strengthening the learning further and connect the activity with feelings of positivity.

Knowledge: knowing what's involved

Knowing and understanding the ingredients, how they connect and inter-relate.

Building up an understanding of any subject[7] is a cumulative process. The subject of *musical performance* in its broadest sense might be said to be made up of three main areas:

[7] A subject can be defined by its constituent parts or ingredients.

- **Technique:** all the skills that are necessary to be able to actually play our instrument or sing.

- **Language:** here I specifically mean understanding and connecting with what we hear (aural) and what we see (notation and 'theory') which particularly allows us to read music meaningfully.

- **Artistry:** knowing how to bring the music we play to life in a creative, evocative, stylistic and imaginative way.

If we do learn (understand) the right ingredient at the right time, in the right order and for the right reasons and if we recognise and comprehend the connection between it and related ingredients (there always are connections), then the learning process is sturdy, reliable, durable and stress-free.

So, what *knowing* is actually involved here? This book is of course dealing specifically with reading and so the relevant ingredients in the actual notation of what we are reading comprise:

- Key and key signatures
- The way we notate pitch and note values
- Rhythm patterns
- Dynamic markings
- Articulation markings
- Tempo and character markings

It's important that the ingredients that make up each of these are *known* and understood as well as possible. If some particular notational symbol is not known there really will be very little we can do as the forward-moving process will hit a block.

Read the following and as you do so, consider *exactly* what is going on in your mind:

Sjónlestur er auðvelt

Now try this:

η ανάγνωση της όρασης είναι εύκολη

The first is Icelandic and the second is Greek. Maybe in the first you might have been making sounds – but they won't really connect with anything we know in English – it is derived from a West Scandinavian language so bears little connection with any shapes or sounds we recognise. The second is Greek but, unless you read Greek, you won't even be able to make the sounds. Both translated mean 'sight-reading is easy' – but it's not if you don't know the language!

There is a discussion about what it is to 'know' something in my book, *Unconditional Teaching*.[8] In brief, if you feel that *you know* that you know something (like your name), then you can feel secure in the knowledge that you do! So it's essential that you do have some understanding of the notation. If there's something you don't understand then seek some help before moving on.

We will be considering key and key signatures and the notation of pitch and rhythm in detail in this book. I will leave knowing how to interpret correctly the various dynamic, articulation, tempo and character markings to you.[9]

[8] *Unconditional Teaching*, chapter 7 (Faber Music)

[9] There are many good theory books and online sites available that will help here including *Improve Your Theory!* (Faber Music)

Technique: how we actually do it

Learning to sight-read simply requires developing the appropriate technique – just as we learn the appropriate technique in order to play an instrument or sing. That is what much of this book is about. Part 3 will look at each of the areas that make up sight-reading technique and will show how each can be developed.

> So, it's the combination of a positive **mindset**, having the appropriate **knowledge** and developing **technique** that will provide the formula to cultivate the confidence to become an effective sight-reader. Hopefully your mindset *will* now be positive! And so we can move on to look at appropriate aspects of knowledge in Part 2 and technique in Part 3.

2 Aspects of knowledge

2.1 The process of reading

We read with our eyes – which are really quite complex parts of our anatomy. For example, each eye consists of more than two million working parts. The eyes collect light but it's the brain that 'sees' and processes around 600 pieces of information per minute. In understanding the reading process, we don't actually need to know anything about how the eyes themselves work but it is both helpful and instructive to have some understanding of the broader processes of reading. Without going into too much scientific detail, this section will look at the basic anatomical and psychological aspects involved.

Our 'field of vision', which is what we see through our eyes, is divided into two areas. The small area of our *central vision* (or fovea) is what we are looking at directly and our *peripheral vision* (the parafovea) is in a sense, what we see 'out of the corner of our eyes'.

When we read words, we *subvocalize* – we hear the words we are reading in our mind's ear. Recent research suggests we even do this when speed reading.[10] In music we need to develop the ability to understand the notational symbols as signifying a sound, which then informs the physical movement to create that sound.

When we read text, we usually process each whole word as a single unit – not through its constituent parts (letters or syllables, for example). Although we do take each letter into account, allowing us to differentiate between words like major and mayor or waited and wasted – where both pairs have just one letter that differs. We need to develop the same important ability to process music in meaningful patterns – like words.

This pattern:

could be the musical equivalent of 'the'. It's a very common, recurring pattern that we find in musical phrases over and over again. You see the notes, you will then know, more or less, what they sound like and then, virtually simultaneously, play them.

[10] 'Speed reading' is a term that refers to an ability to read quickly. It was coined in the late 1950s and has received mixed reactions. This article presents a very reasoned argument: "So Much to Read, So Little Time", *Psychological Science in the Public Interest* (2016). See also: Rayner, K. *Eye movements in reading and information processing: 20 years of research.* Psychological Bulletin, 124(3), 372–422 (1998).

In developing good sight-reading technique, the reading process should look something like this:

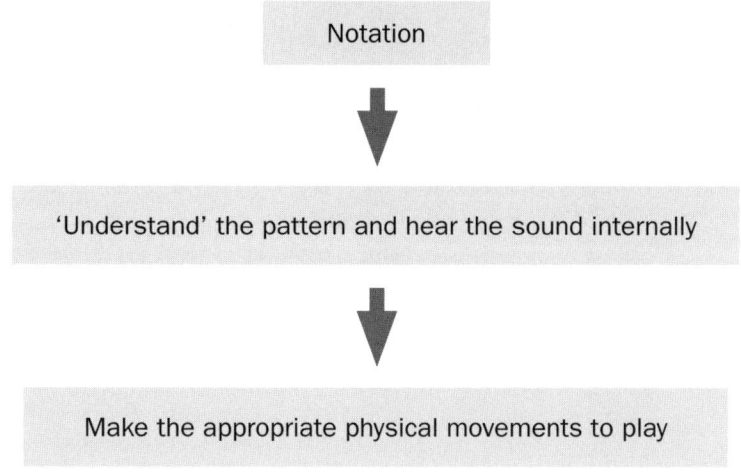

Rather than this:

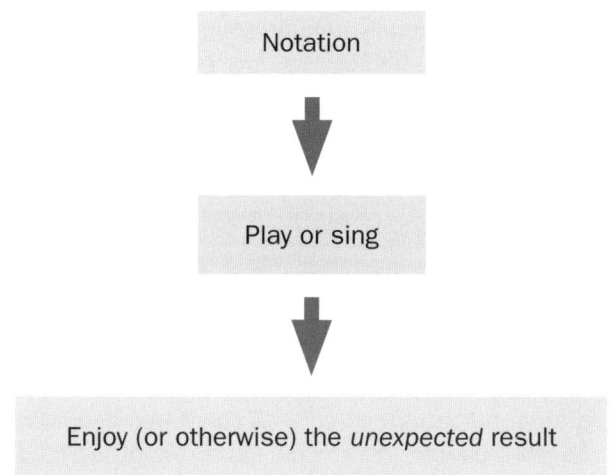

Of course, this process happens in a very short space of time.

As we read, our eyes are constantly moving rapidly around the page, though (we hope) that movement is mostly confined to the actual region where we are reading. These rapid eye movements are called *saccades* or saccadic movement.[11] Each of these movements can happen in as little as 20–30 milliseconds.[12] So theoretically we could move our eyes literally hundreds of times a second. Which of course we don't! In reality, we move our eyes about three (or sometimes maybe four) times a second.

[11] The word *saccade* comes from old French, meaning 'a jerking movement'.

[12] Dennis F. Fisher, Richard A. Monty, John W. Senders *Eye Movements: Cognition and Visual Perception*, Routledge (1981).

Try this experiment:

> Ask a friend to gaze into your eyes as you read a few sentences in your head from this page. Then swap over and discuss what you see. You'll notice that the eye movement is jerky – or *saccadic*. With short stops in between called *fixations*, which is when the eyes are temporarily motionless to input the data (i.e. what we are presently and directly looking at) and then sending that information to the brain for processing. This all happens very quickly!

As we develop sight-reading technique we learn to process more and more in each very short fixation. In a way, musical patterns begin to take on a meaning something akin to vocabulary. With a little practice and thought, patterns such as these…

…and the virtually infinite number like them, will be read in a single, short fixation – just like you are reading these words.

Convergence insufficiency

With normal sight we have what is termed binocular single vision (or BSV). When this is working normally, the two eyes converge and can focus on a close object, such as words, a book, computer, tablet or a phone, for example. *Convergence insufficiency* is a condition where there is a problem with eye-brain co-ordination and so the eyes don't work naturally together. Symptoms may manifest in eye strain, double vision, headaches, a sense of the print moving on the page, blurred vision and loss of place when reading. If children are seen regularly to shut or cover one eye, rub their eyes or squint this may be the cause. It is said that about 15% of people have convergence insufficiency, often without their knowledge.[13] This will certainly have an effect on sight-reading – or indeed reading music in general.

If you suspect a student may have convergence insufficiency or any other visual difficulty, do refer them to an optometrist or eye doctor. There are a number of effective ways in which it can be treated. If the symptoms are more that the notes are jumping out of sequence then it may be a sign of dyspraxia or dyslexia; there are specialist optometrists who can assess the condition and help.

[13] nei.nih.gov/learn-about-eye-health/eye-conditions-and-diseases/convergence-insufficiency

2.2 Introducing pulse, rhythm and pitch

These are the three main ingredients that require instant and intuitive understanding. We have to 'know' them (and *know* that we know them!) for really secure and confident sight-reading to develop.

Pulse

Pulse is the single most important requirement behind successful sight-reading, because without it, reliable and efficient sight-reading is never going to work. So let's consider the important question:

> **What does having a sense of pulse mean?**

You will remember our definition of pulse as the division of time (in its non-musical sense) into regular units. We have to develop an ability to feel these regular divisions naturally. We have to develop an inner metronome that has, as near as possible, the regularity and security of a physical metronome.

Some people can clap a steady pulse naturally. We all have a physical pulse – our heartbeat.[14] If you wish to develop this skill, try this exercise. Having a friend along will be very helpful but you can do this on your own:

Set a metronome at 60 bpm (that's one beat per second) and clap along with it. After a while switch the metronome off and keep clapping. After a bit longer switch it back on again and see if your clapping (your pulse) is still regular and in time with the metronome. Repeat as necessary – in most cases, a week or two of regular work should make a noticeable difference. Try this exercise at many different speeds.

When you feel confident that you can clap a steady pulse, try this sequence of exercises, moving seamlessly from one to the next:

- Clap and count aloud (at about 100 bpm) four bars of four beats *(one-two-three-four one-two-three-four, etc)*
- Stop clapping but continue to count a further four bars aloud
- Whisper the next four bars
- Silently mouth the next four bars
- Still counting the numbers, hear the next four bars internally
- Replace the numbers with a pulse: a mental sensation of the counting.

[14] A normal, resting heart will beat, steadily, between about 60 and 100 bpm. Our pulse rate refers to the number of times the arteries expand and contract in response to the pumping action of the heart – also measured as a bpm. So the pulse rate is in fact exactly equal to the heartbeat.

You have developed a *sense of pulse*. Be aware of this sense of pulse whenever you are playing. It is the fundamental foundation that will underpin your reading and sight-reading.

> It's essential – it REALLY is – that before playing or singing we set up the appropriate pulse in our minds. Maybe hearing one bar of pulse internally. Beginners should be encouraged and taught to do this as often as possible. In an ideal world – every time they are about to play. Ultimately this will become intuitive. But it won't (except in a small number who seem to get this instinctively) if we don't make it a priority in teaching and learning.

Rhythm

We now need to ask the question:

> **What does having a sense of rhythm mean?**

Here, we are using the word rhythm in its meaning as a succession or pattern of notes with particular values of duration. The answer then is *being able to decode those patterns instantly.* That's certainly an essential ability in the development of accurate and fluent sight-reading.

The secret of doing this lies in the simple and vital art of *subdivision*.

But in order to do this, we need to develop further our ability to internalise music accurately and vividly.

The inner ear

We can all hear music internally – using what some call our musical *inner ear*.[15] Hear 'Happy Birthday' or any tune you know well, *in your head*.[16] You are using your inner ear. Hear it again and notice that you're hearing the melody, almost certainly the harmony and of course the note lengths or rhythm.

Now hear it yet again and see what you can work out from your own *inner performance* of Happy Birthday. For example, can you work out:

- The time signature.
- On which beat of the bar it begins.
- The rhythmic patterns – of the opening two notes, for example, or any of it.
- The scale of the key you are hearing – not the *actual* scale (G major for example – unless you have perfect pitch) but the sequence of notes in their scale pattern. Knowing that the first time you hear 'to' and the last note are both the tonic (or first note of the scale and key) will help.
- On which note of the scale it begins.
- If you know harmony and chord labels, can you work out what the chords are?

[15] From a scientific point of view this is different from the anatomical *inner ear*.

[16] Hearing music in your head is sometimes labelled *audiation*. There are a small number who have particular hearing conditions making the perception and processing of music potentially unfeasible: hyperacusis, tinnitus and Meniere's Disease among them. There are good online sites that explain these conditions. Those with dyslexia may also struggle with reading as the left occipito-temporal cortex (which links a written word to its spoken equivalent) may be malfunctioning. They may be more aurally oriented, and may learn better by reading aloud or listening. Some research suggests that for dyslexics, rhythm may be more complex to process than pitch.

Are you hearing it played by a particular instrument? Or sung? Can you re-hear it played by a full symphony orchestra with added percussion… maybe put a triumphant cymbal clash and a drum roll on the final note!

It's rare not to possess a musical inner ear and with practice it can be refined and developed significantly.

Subdivision

Once you feel that you can sense and sustain a steady pulse the ability to subdivide that pulse can be developed. It's a vitally important ability and there is a lot more about developing this in practical ways in Part 3.

But here's a start: hear this 'pulse' internally and, in this case, hear the line as being played strongly and resonantly as if on a bass drum at about 80 bpm:

Now, at the same tempo hear internally the upper line as if played on a crisp side drum simultaneously with the lower line:

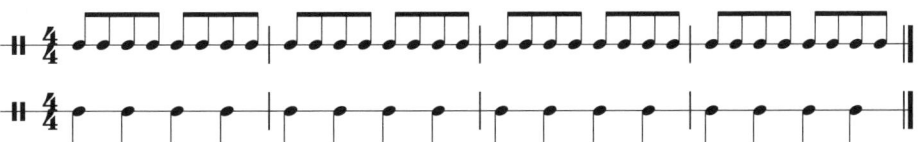

You are subdividing the pulse. With this understanding comes the ability to bring most rhythms correctly and confidently to life – and you will be conscious that you are doing it deliberately both accurately and knowingly.

Ultimately you will be able to develop an inner metronome that is *always* sensing pulse and the subdivision of that pulse if and as necessary – we shall explore how this can be done in Part 3.

Pitch

When it comes to perceiving and processing pitch in the context of reading there are two basic elements that are necessary to know. And knowing these elements, preferably, in that know that you know them sort of way!

- The letter names of notes – and we have to know these without having to think about them or work them out. If you or a student are still at the *Every Good Boy Does Fine* stage, work at trying to make the written note and its name an immediate connection.[17]
- Where that note is to be found on your instrument or, if you are a singer, where the note is in relation to the previous and next note.

[17] Music note flashcards are a good way to help here.

The next stage is to begin to perceive these notes as *patterns*, which will happen as soon as there is more than one note on its own. Look at the following pattern:

We can notice (and therefore know) a number of things about this pattern:

- It's an ascending pattern
- The notes move up in a stepwise manner
- The pattern represents the first 5 notes of the scale (and therefore key) of C major
- We may instinctively know how to play them on our instrument
- We may instinctively know what the pattern sounds like – without necessarily playing them or even hearing them in our musical inner ear.

Look at it again, making sure you have acknowledged, understood and processed each of the points in relation to the pattern.

These patterns are the musical equivalent of words. The more immediate the process of perceiving musical patterns like words becomes, the more fluent the reading will be.

Here's another pattern:

- The notes go up and come down
- All the intervals are skips of a third
- The pattern represents a tonic triad of C major
- We may instinctively know how to play the pattern on our instrument
- We may know what the pattern sounds like – again without necessarily playing the notes or even hearing them in our musical inner ear.

Naturally the patterns may be a lot more complex and not relate specifically to regular forms or configurations of notes. Nevertheless, having this awareness – always to be on the lookout and ultimately to be able to process such patterns instinctively – will clearly result in much more fluent and accurate reading. We will consider how this is actually developed in Part 3.

2.3 Why all this is important and what some are seeing

Having this basic understanding will be very helpful as a foundation for building a really sturdy and reliable sight-reading technique. But it certainly doesn't all have to be thoroughly digested before we really get going. Much of it can be picked up, absorbed and integrated along the way.

But unfortunately there is some teaching and learning going on that results in major knowledge gaps, giving us little doubt as to why some might develop a fear of and consider sight-reading a near-impossible task. I'm often asked to give dedicated sight-reading lessons and, in the case of violinists for example, I sometimes use the following as an opening exercise. I always begin with some questions to see where we are and the answers can be very revealing:

All these answers come from lessons I've given:

1 **Q:** What difference can you see between the first bar and last bar?
   A: *The last bar has two lines at the end.*

2 **Q:** Are there any similarities between the first 3 bars?
   A: *No*

3 **Q:** So what is the difference you see between bar 1 and 3?
   A: *Bar one has a C in it.*

4 **Q:** Do you know what the C is?
   A: *It means C major (another answer was: it's C for 'count')*

5 **Q:** Are any bars the same?
   A: *No*

6 **Q:** Is bar 1 repeated?
   A: *No*

7 **Q:** Can you say anything about high and low notes?
   A: *Bar 2 has the highest notes*

8 **Q:** Is that bow sign on the second note an up or a down bow?
   A: *It's a down bow because it's pointing down*

All the answers are quite understandable and, in their own way, logical and indeed interesting. In question 1, although the notes are the same and the only difference is one rhythmic change, bar 1 looks different because it also has a clef and time signature and the final bar has a double barline. Similar reasons would explain the answer in question 2: the student is distracted by other elements. The responses to questions 3, 5 and 6 are further proof of the misunderstandings surrounding additional elements seen in those bars. Question 4 shows lack of knowledge of what the time signature is. The answer to question 7 is due to the stem in bar 2 being the highest point – and the answer to question 8 is quite convincing! The problem is that the answers demonstrate serious gaps in the correct interpretation of the notation from a musical point of view. A player setting off to do some reading with this degree of confusion in their minds is going to find any attempt actually to play the music a considerable struggle.

The ultimate intention is to *know* that you know most of the concepts and information we've explored in this chapter. Those that you don't will inevitably (with practice and thought) become part of your knowledge and instinct as we now proceed to develop this technique in Part 3.

3 Developing sight-reading technique

> In Part 3 we are going to see that sight-reading is a skill that can be developed – just as we develop our skill or technique in playing an instrument or singing. There are a number of individual areas that we can work on, each with their own journey, which grows with clear discernible progress. These *together* contribute to the ability to process notation and therefore to sight-read – incrementally and so at *any level* – with accuracy, fluency and confidence. Remember, whatever level you are, you can be good *at that level*.

It's important, as each of these techniques are being worked through, to replace any negative or over-rigorous self-criticism with a more self-aware, observational and objective approach.[18] This is the sort of thought process we should be aspiring to:

[18] I call this the '00' (double-0) Mindset – being observational and objective about what we do. Simply notice what you did and why you did it and decide what you will do next – all without making personal judgements. There is more about this in *Unconditional Teaching*, Chapter 10.

> This is what I did…
> ▼
> …with this result…
> ▼
> …I'd prefer a different result, so
> ▼
> …now I'll try doing it like this instead

As progress is being made, keep a keen awareness of what has been learnt and what is now known – and know, when the moment has been reached, that we *know* that we know.

In this way we are really building up confidence in the learning.

3.1 Knowledge and deepening understanding of ingredients

This is more an approach to general musical development and learning rather than a technique in itself. But in understanding the importance of knowing what the ingredients are, learners will set up the potential for really effective progress.

The actual process of learning is, as you would imagine, a complex one.[19] But as far as we need to understand it, we (or a student) gradually learn the particular ingredients and information, and the appropriate skills that together add up to playing or singing music. Eventually, and with *thorough* learning (through lots of practice and making many connections via the Simultaneous Learning Musical Map of the World), this information and these skills end up in the long-term memory, which we draw on when undertaking a new task (like sight-reading).

[19] There are many books and online sites that will explain learning in considerable detail should you be interested.

Read the instruction in this box:

> Count silently to eight at ♩ = 60 and then, at the same tempo, snap your fingers four times with a *crescendo*.
>
> Now cover this instruction up or look away and perform the task.

I suspect you managed that without too much difficulty or stress. But let's see what you already knew that allowed you to do that.

You knew:

- How to count up to eight and how to do it 'silently'
- What that musical code ♩ = 60 and the expression 'at the same tempo' meant
- How to snap your fingers
- What *crescendo* meant and how to control one technically in your snapping!

And you possibly did it from memory. All the appropriate ingredients, both knowledge and skills were known – they were somewhere in your long-term memory. You drew on them sub-consciously and carried out the task. It's really just the same in sight-reading.

Any piece or song is similarly made up of a collection of ingredients. It's essential that you know, understand and can manage these when preparing a performance. They come in three areas: technique, language and artistry. Be aware of them and aware that you know how to manage each (and know that you know!). Not only will things improve at a surprisingly fast pace but it will also generate the brain space to include area three – the artistic area: playing or singing with musical expression. Something that often gets overlooked when sight-reading.

In your general practice, whenever you are preparing to play or sing from notation, *always* scan through the music first and ask yourself the following questions.

- **Technique** – do I have complete technical control over everything here? And of course if not, then that's what I practise!

- **Language** – do I really know how to decode all the notation: the key (pitch) and all the rhythmic content? If not, then any gaps should be carefully filled before playing.

- **Artistry** – how will the music be brought to life with appropriate character? Are all the markings understood and is the intention to make the most of them part of my thinking?

If the first two areas are secure you will have the necessary brain space to realise the artistic aspect. And, of course, all of this will have a marked effect on your sight-reading.

As you begin a new piece, make a list of all the ingredients, tick off those you do know and then each of the rest as they become fully understood and mastered.

> I sometimes ask what the difference is between a beginner and a more advanced musician. The answer is simply that the more advanced musician knows, understands and is more familiar with *more* ingredients. Make sure each ingredient is really known and nothing will inhibit as much progress as you desire.

3.2 Hearing it in our heads

Just as you are hearing these words in your head as you read them, it is important to have the same ability when you read music. This is a technique that can be developed.

Always try to make the connection from the written notation to internalising the sound of that notation. For a beginner this can be done from the very first encounter with notation.[20] And so the student:

[20] See also Chapter 4.3, page 74.

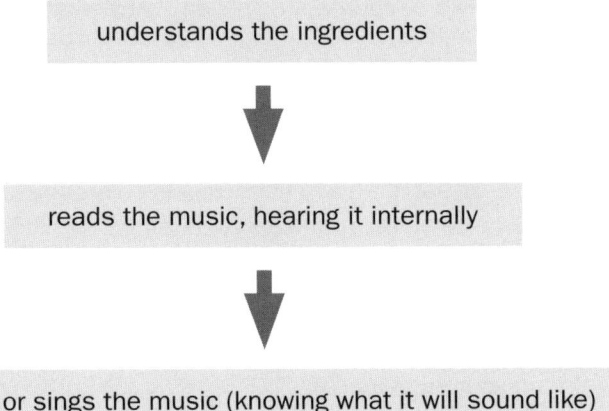

Those taught in this way will never find reading music a problem.

For a more advanced student who has not been taught in this way and feels doing so is something that seems akin to climbing a very high mountain (which it isn't, by the way!), try this:

> Find a beginners' book (whatever level you or your student happens to be at now) and start again, from the very first stage! Look at each exercise and piece and read it, being aware that you are reading it. Read it, *hearing the music in your head* as you do so. Then play it to check you were right. You almost always will be! Go through the entire book in this way. You'll soon realise that you really are *reading* music!

Make part of your regular practice simply sitting in a comfortable chair with some music and reading it in your head. Choose pieces or songs that are both familiar and unfamiliar. With unfamiliar music you should be 100% accurate with the rhythm, though the pitch might not be quite so accurate – it doesn't matter. And remember to hear the dynamics! You will improve. It's a technique that everyone can develop.

3.3 Brain processing speed and pattern recognition

There is quite a body of research showing that we can develop our brain processing speed. The playing of certain video games has now been proven to reduce reaction times without reducing accuracy.[21]

In one way or another our brains are processing an enormous amount of information at an enormously fast speed. Consider the huge number of tasks demanded by our bodies in everyday living; the process of breathing for example – which happens without any *conscious* processing – together with all the other things we may be consciously doing or experiencing at any one moment. In fact, the human body can send about 11 million bits per second to the brain for processing.

Without going into too much detail (although the details really are fascinating!) information is received by and subsequently stored in the brain in the form of 'bits' which is the most basic measure of a piece of information. Eight bits form a byte – a unit we know well from computer terminology. The human brain has, on average, the capacity to store about 2.5 million gigabytes of information in the memory. That's a lot! Recent research suggests that the human brain *actually* processes about 126 bits per second which is considered to be the *speed of thought*.[22]

That's more than enough for successful sight-reading!

Maybe even more important to know is that the brain continually has the ability to learn and grow, a process known as brain plasticity.[23]

The actual processing speed is the rate at which you input information, make sense of it, and then make your response. It is a central requirement of sight-reading technique and, like all matters of technique, it is entirely possible to develop. As we've seen when discussing eye movement (which is a sequence of saccades and fixations), our eyes work rather like a camera – and the more we can absorb during each fixation (or snapshot) the more fluent our sight-reading will become. What we do see sometimes will be an instantly recognisable pattern (maybe based on a scale or an arpeggio) or it may be a less familiar shape. Learning to improve our speed of recognising patterns and processing them: i.e. the journey from input (seeing) to output (playing or singing) is one that is very important and can be developed.[24]

[21] If you're interested in the science do read *Increasing Speed of Processing With Action Video Games* in *Current Directions in Psychological Science*, 2009.

[22] sciencefocus.com/the-human-body/what-is-the-speed-of-thought

[23] Recent research has found that neuroplasticity (the scientific term for brain plasticity) doesn't necessarily decline with age, especially if the brain is kept active. Processing music is a very good way to keep it active. For more information see *The aging mind: neuroplasticity in response to cognitive training* Denise C. Park, National Library of Medicine, 2013.

[24] This is known as the *eye-hand span* which is in effect the distance in time between the eye's reading and the hand's playing. In some research (see[22]) the eyes were about two beats ahead of the fingers.

Do practise your scales!

Scales, and all their various related patterns, are the basis of much musical vocabulary. So many patterns that make up so much music in so many styles and genres, are related to scale patterns. They also help all kinds of technical work (changing hand position, shifting and using alternative fingerings, for example) and key familiarity. Do practise them from notation as regularly as possible. Maybe one or two each practice session. They're not boring or tedious – especially if they are approached with a positive attitude and an understanding of what they truly represent: the pitch patterns from which so much music grows.

The brain processing speed app

If you work systematically at the Brain Processing Speed element on the sight-reading app (see page 8) you can develop this important area of your sight-reading technique.

Follow the set-up instructions found on the app carefully. To begin, use simple ingredients to create your exercises. Work out what you find achievable: not *too* simple but by no means anything that might cause you any more than a slender challenge. Maybe one bar, made up of a straightforward rhythm, then set the app to display each exercise for between two and four seconds (four seconds is the maximum the app can display each exercise). If you've managed to find just the right ingredients to begin your development, enjoy the exercises and then next session reduce the time very slightly – so you'll hardly notice the difference. If you began with two seconds, maybe reduce to 1.9 seconds. And in the next session, reduce the time a little more. With patience you will, almost imperceptibly, be improving your brain processing speed.

Then start another sequence – maybe the following day, week or month, it doesn't matter – with more notes, a more complex rhythmic pattern or a new key. Very gradually reduce the processing time. The number of variations that the app can create is virtually infinite and, with appropriate patience, you will gradually develop your ability to read patterns quicker. Simultaneously, and in a sense without realising it, you are also developing the skill of temporarily memorising these patterns (using your working memory).[25] You will be developing your sight-reading technique in a very real and perceptible way.

There are two ways to use these exercises:

1. Recall the exercise immediately in your mind's eye – in effect putting it into your short-term memory – then compare what you remembered when the music reappears.
2. Process the music and immediately play it. This will develop the eye-hand span which is in effect the time between the eye's reading and the hand(s) playing.

Press go and enjoy the ride!

[25] The simplest definition of working memory (which, interestingly, involves at least five separate brain areas anatomically!) is the holding of information for a brief time to be used in the processing of mental tasks.

Pianists will note that there is not an option for reading two staves simultaneously. This is a deliberate decision based on the actual visible area available when using our central vision. Our central vision will only be able to take in the details of one line at a time per fixation. Therefore, the important skill to develop is the processing of a single stave. In piano reading, the eyes are constantly darting from one stave to the other – building up a picture, in your mind, of both staves. The quicker the information is processed the more efficiently you will be reading. This, in conjunction with the development of peripheral vision (see over), will create the ideal conditions for developing fluent sight-reading technique on all instruments and voices.

3.4 Peripheral vision and looking ahead

You may have heard about the extraordinary skills of some musicians who evidently can read 5, 10, 15 bars ahead or even more. Let's consider this skill now, and how you can develop it as part of your sight-reading technique. It links in with and follows on from the previous technique, the ability to process short patterns in a fixation which also involves the simultaneous memorising of those patterns. This allows the reader to look ahead to the next pattern whilst playing or singing the previous one (or 'developing the eye-hand span').

There are, fundamentally, two aspects to our vision. Our central vision is what we are looking at directly, simultaneously picking up the details. And our peripheral vision is what we 'see' around that central vision – in other words, everything else that is in our visual field but that we are not looking at directly.

Try this experiment:

> Choose something to look at – a door handle, a particular book in the bookcase, an ornament on top of the piano, your clarinet mouthpiece sitting in its clarinet case. You are using your central vision to look at that object. Now, without changing or moving your gaze, use your brain to start noticing things contained in your peripheral vision: the rest of the door; something by or beyond the door; another book; a pile of music on the piano; other sections of the clarinet. Now you are becoming aware of your peripheral vision. If you repeated a simple exercise like this every day you would begin to go some way to training your brain to be more aware of what's going on around your central vision. Drivers do this all the time.

Here's another activity you can do to develop this ability with a pack of cards. Doing this with a student (or teacher) or friend will make it more fun, but it's entirely possible to do on your own.

Put two cards next to each other with a small gap inbetween. Look, using your central vision, at the first card and, without changing your gaze, see if you can work out what the second card is. Keep changing the second card. Place it slightly further away from the first each time. Then try it with three cards.

You will already see the benefits of developing peripheral vision as a sight-reader. As you are reading, your brain will begin to process what's coming in the next fixation – even though you won't actually be there yet. The influence on fluency is significant.

The second element on the sight-reading web app is designed to develop this skill. As you did in the Brain Processing section, set up the first bar with as much detail as you like and then decide whether you'd like 1, 2, 3 or 4 notes to appear in the second bar. Then set the sequence going and, using your central vision to look directly at the first bar, see whether you can read whatever comes in the next bar. Begin with one note in the second bar and gradually reduce the time and increase the number of notes as you grow in skill and confidence. You are developing your skill to look ahead.

Consciously looking ahead

The skill outlined above is essentially an unconscious one. Your brain will already be assimilating and processing something of what is coming along next before your central vision actually inputs the material for immediate playing.

In association with this there are certain patterns or ingredients to look out for that signal opportunities where you can *consciously* make yourself look ahead.

If you notice any of the following, make a *conscious effort* to look ahead:

- Repeated notes
- Longer notes
- Repeated chords or chord progressions
- Repeated rhythmic or melodic patterns
- Rests
- Ends of phrases

Again, in time, this will become instinctive.

Thus, the *technique* of looking ahead has become a part of the sight-reading developmental process. Both your sub-conscious and conscious awareness of the process are now part of the journey towards fluent and accurate sight-reading.

Covering and uncovering

While a student is sight-reading (or just reading), teachers have sometimes adopted the technique of covering the notes (with a small piece of card, maybe) once those notes have been played to encourage the eyes to look ahead. Other teachers cover the notes *about* to be played and let the music unfold – as though drawing the eyes forward and so causing the player to look ahead. One teacher I know gently taps with a finger on the music just a few notes ahead of what is being played.

Personally, I slightly prefer the second method as the eyes often make very brief backward movements which seem to give the player a certain security about what they've just played. But both, used occasionally, can be helpful and may encourage some interesting discussion on the process during the lesson.

3.5 Walking the course[26]

[26] I've borrowed this phrase from the world of horse racing and show jumping. Riders will *walk the course* beforehand to become familiar with it and notice any particular or relevant details.

Another way of developing the 'snapshot' idea (the amount of information we can understand and take in on one fixation) and something that will develop an intuitive and comprehensive awareness of what you are seeing is to 'walk the course'. This is probably best done without your instrument and sitting in a comfortable chair. It will also further strengthen appropriate musical connections (particularly with theory and the notation). Again, this is something that would benefit from regular practice.

Choose a phrase (or longer passage) from the piece or song you are about to read and then, reading from left to right, describe and explain what you see as a kind of narrative. Working together with a student (or a teacher) would be ideal. Look at the following example and make some notes on exactly what you see (either in your mind or write them down):

Your thoughts would ideally go something like this:

- It begins with a two-note slurred pattern where the second note is a tone lower (or one note lower) than the first. Maybe add that the notes are E and D and each are one beat crotchets (quarter notes).
- This is followed by an upward arpeggio (or chord) of C major. For students who may not yet be able to label the patterns in this rather more abstract way, maybe they can be encouraged to describe the pattern as a series of jumps that mostly skip over one note except the one that skips over two.
- Then follows another two-note slurred pattern which is the same as the opening pattern but an octave higher.
- And it concludes with a descending chord pattern of C major – the opposite of the ascending pattern in bar 1.

This kind of thinking makes lots of appropriate connections and will allow the eye/brain system to read and perceive the patterns in four short fixations:

With this kind of practice, the brain will intuitively begin to make all those connections and if all the appropriate playing technique is assimilated (the best fingering to use, for example) then the passage will be read and played both fluently and accurately.

Read this passage:

Almost certainly you will only need two fixations to process the information, again encouraging a much greater fluency.[27]

Here's an example for piano where the eyes will necessarily have to track vertically as well as horizontally.[28]

[27] This technique is sometimes called *chunking*. It's a term, used in cognitive psychology, to describe a process where 'pieces' of information are combined to create a meaningful 'whole' which can positively impact short-term memory retention and form the basis of what we can input in each fixation.

[28] Some very interesting research into eye movement in piano reading has been reported in 'The Performance of Music' by John Sloboda in *The Musical Mind*, Oxford, 1985 and more recently, by Truitt et al: 'The perceptual span and the eye–hand span in sight-reading music' in *Visual Cognition*, Volume 4, Number 2, 1997.

Firstly, a quick skim through might generate the following commentary:

- The passage is based on a melody in the right hand supported by a two-note harmony in the left hand, one chord per bar.
- It begins with a unison G.
- The notes making up the melody in the right-hand bar 1 are all in the arpeggio of G major.
- This is followed by a chord of D major with a scale passage that ascends and descends.
- The next bar repeats the left-hand fifth. The held note in the right hand lowers to a C (creating a 7th chord) and the melody is almost the same in rhythm and pitch – but it ends on an A leading to the final bar.
- The final bar is the same as the first bar.

Although it is impossible to predict or control the way individuals might sequence their eye movement, we could make an informed guess that the first fixation takes in the right hand first bar, with peripheral vision noticing the left hand is also playing Gs. Maybe a quick saccadic movement to the left-hand line to check. Then back to the right hand, and with the background knowledge that the harmony has changed to D major, a saccadic movement to the left hand which will confirm the prediction. And so on…! In practice, the eye movement may go something like this:

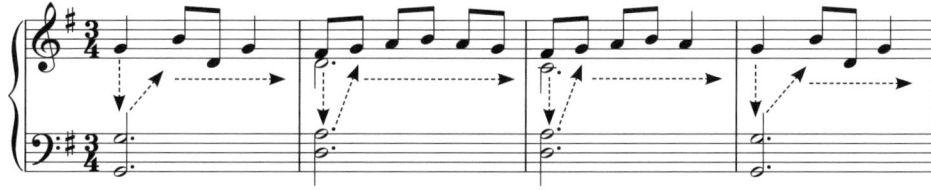

When reading contrapuntal music, the eyes are having to make a more complex journey. But in order to initiate this journey, the player needs to acknowledge that the music *is* contrapuntal! Another example of the importance of being able to draw on background knowledge and understanding.

The eye movement, in the following more contrapuntal example, is maybe something like that shown below. Though a brief fixation on the right hand 'D' would probably begin the journey, because the moving part begins in the left hand, the eyes would probably be drawn there as the point of departure:

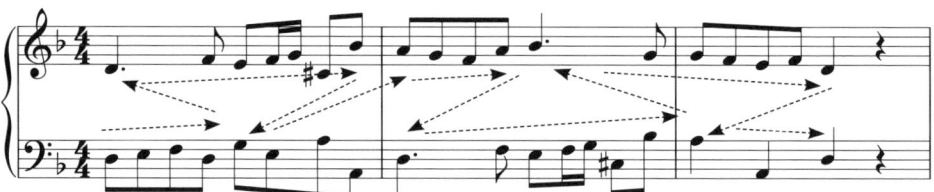

Obviously, we don't instruct our students, or indeed ourselves, to read (move our eyes) like this in any detail. Our eyes will make their movements instinctively and it simply happens automatically. We can't consciously prepare our eye movement or expect the eyes to move in a certain way. But with awareness and the development of all the related aspects, the actual reading is clearly going to become much more efficient and fluent.

Developing musical instinct

There is an associated thought worth bearing in mind, which is related specifically to sight-reading in the sense of the *very first time a piece is read* – maybe in an exam, an orchestral rehearsal or as a répétiteur, perhaps.

Read the following:

> It was played really acccurately: and the musical shape and phasing was outstanding. It was never out of tune, in fact both the intonation and artculation was prefect.

There were a number of small errors in both the spelling (four in fact) as well as one grammatical slip. Read it again if you didn't spot them all. But the point is that the sense was completely secure.

If you were reading the passage above (written for the clarinet) and instinctively knew the patterns (C major arpeggios, dominant 7ths on G, various diminished 7ths, partial scale in thirds towards the end) but, in the performance put some of the notes in a slightly different order, and maybe played something like this:

...the musical meaning is still very much there and the patterns lead on in musical and logical ways.

Imagine this as a few bars of a left-hand piano line:

As long as you process the correct harmony there are many ways of playing this passage which would be entirely acceptable in performance. There are all sorts of 'edits' possible to make it simpler to control – especially at speed. Fewer notes in the chords and smaller leaps, for example.

This version, where the hand hardly changes position, would do perfectly well in giving the same musical effect:

Developing your musical instinct by making strong connections with your understanding of the ingredients (we'll come back to this again in the section on Improvisation) is certainly beneficial.

Making 'walking the course' a regular part of practice will thus be very helpful in developing your sight-reading technique.

Here's an activity that can be attempted at all levels and brings many of the techniques behind successful sight-reading together. I call it **Activity X** – an exercise in creative fusion. It's a creative activity that can be done as an exam is approaching and will exercise the musical mind in a number of very helpful ways.

Choose a piece to sight-read and 'walk the course' carefully. Then read it through internally as best you can, much in the way you prepare a piece. But instead of sight-reading the piece, close the book and create your own piece, mirroring the written piece to some degree and certainly using all the piece's ingredients – but not worrying about trying to reproduce it accurately.

This activity will exercise memory, understanding of the ingredients and predictive skills. It's a very holistic and musical activity. Afterwards read the piece in the normal way, mentally comparing it either as you're playing it or afterwards, to your Activity X version.

3.6 Key awareness

When sight-reading, and indeed when re-reading a piece played a number of times already, it's essential to understand and remember the key and develop the skill of *thinking in a key*. Many players simply live in C major and then try to 'remember' the appropriate sharps and flats. This puts a real strain on the working memory, leaving little brain space for all the other ingredients.

The solution lies partly in scales. Again, I would urge all musicians to make friends with scales and their related patterns.[29] Not only arpeggios, dominant 7th and diminished chords, but, for example, also knowing about scales in thirds, and each key's close relations – the dominant, sub-dominant and relative minor. So, when you're about to play in a particular key, allow its relative keys to flash across your mind: for G major, you'd think C and D majors and E minor. Making that connection could turn out to be very useful. But beware of that often-used circle of fifths diagram so many of us were brought up on (the one with all the key signatures included)! Actually, for many, it's rather intimidating and complex-looking; imaginative teachers might like to try to create alternative ways of introducing the idea like the simplified version below.

[29] This is slightly different for singers, unless they have perfect pitch, so they don't really need to practise scales in all keys (except maybe for technical purposes). But being aware of the *shape* of all scale patterns is still very important.

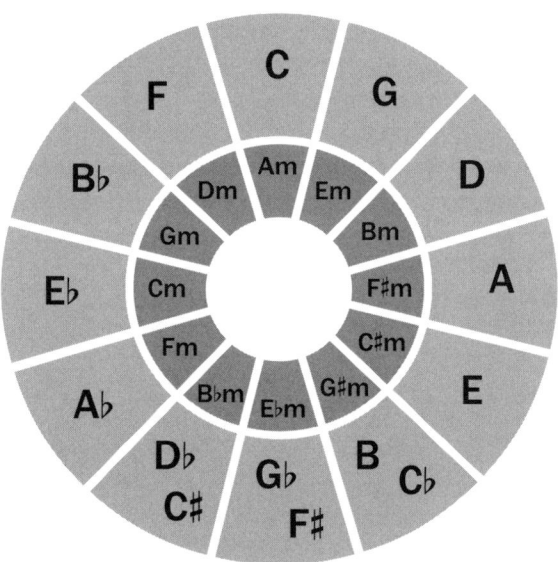

Do play and study scales and all their related patterns from notation. And don't just use the notation as a kind of *aide-mémoire* but really read and process the patterns with a high degree of awareness.

Additionally try to 'see' your instrument in the key in which you are playing. See the piano 'in D major' – see and imagine the notes of D major standing out:

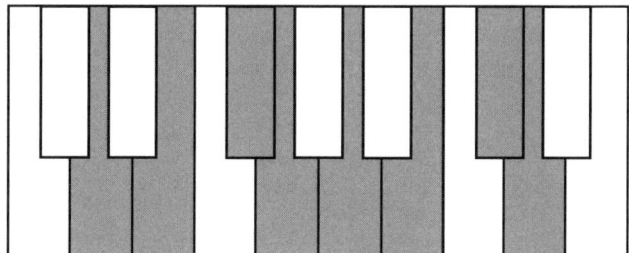

Have a go at seeing and feeling the arpeggio in this way too. On other instruments, feel the violin fingerboard *in the key* with a sense of the appropriate finger patterns – or feel the sequence of fingerings on your flute or clarinet.

Think about the particular personality traits that *are* a particular key and how they relate to your instrument. Here are three that distinguish the key of E major:

- It begins on E
- It has four sharps and…
- Those sharps come in two sets of pairs.

Spend some time considering the concept of key and what *thinking in a key* means to you.

Transposing

Transposing is a skill that in the main is limited to orchestral clarinet, trumpet and horn players and organists (sometimes also pianists who are accompanying choirs and singers). But it can be very useful for players of all instruments to have a go at it. Taking a few bars from a piece you're playing, or a dedicated sight-reading exercise, and transpose it (for example) up a tone. The real benefit here will be gained by *thinking in the new key* and mapping the *patterns* you're reading onto the new key. So in the example below, don't think 'the first note up a tone is G and then the next note up a tone is B and the next D…' and so on. Rather think *in G major* and see the shape as a triad on the tonic note of the new key and then allow your brain to process all the shapes in the new key. Carry on in this way rather than trying to think what each note would become, which is a much more laborious and unmusical process:

Now try transposing into other keys. Here's an example for transposing up a fifth:

And here's the transposed version to check:

Try thinking of all keys (and scales) simply as transpositions of each other. There is really only one major scale!

This activity will help to develop both your pattern recognition and understanding of *thinking in a key* to a significant extent.

> So, when you're about to play in a particular key, switch on your 'thinking in the key' mechanism, which is really an instant combination of all the ideas above, taking into account:
>
> - What are the personality traits of the key?
> - Can I see the scale/arpeggio flash across my mind?
> - Can I feel the patterns on my instrument?
> - Being aware of the related keys.

3.7 Subdivision

The one-and-a-half syndrome

Here's a question:

> How do you count a dotted crotchet*?

* Or dotted quarter note.

On too many occasions I have heard this answer:

> It's one and a half.

Of course, we do know what that answer means – but how *do* you count one and a half beats? And how do you teach a student to count *one and a half*?

It's impossible, really.

To understand how to count a dotted crotchet* we need to teach and learn the inestimable art of **subdivision**. Have a look back at page 29 for an introduction to the art. We now need to develop it as a permanent part of our sight-reading skill-set.

Here are some activities to practise. They will assist you in developing the technique of subdivision.

> 1. On a table or any flat surface or piano lid, tap a ♩ pulse with one hand and the subdivision of that pulse (♫) with the other.
>
>   Stop tapping and continue to hear the sounds internally – maybe assign a different sound to each (bass drum and side drum, for example). Try to alter the dynamic of each sound in your head: a loud pulse and quiet subdivision and then the other way around.

> 2. Repeat, exchanging the ♫ subdivision for ♬ and then triplets.

3. With your pulse sounding clearly in your head, hear both these lines internally and simultaneously and repeat many times:

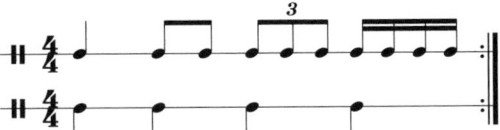

4. If you are out walking at a steady pace (which then becomes the pulse), try subdividing that pulse into the various subdivisions (♩♫, ♬ and triplets) in your head. Each step represents a beat.

5. Then try varying the subdivision on each step.

6. Play a scale thinking a different subdivision on each note. Here are two examples:

Now play the scale with the rhythms, feeling the internal pulse strongly:

And then repeat often, altering the order of the rhythmic patterns.

7. Here's a good exercise to try out your internal subdivision. Hear, internally, this pulse with this 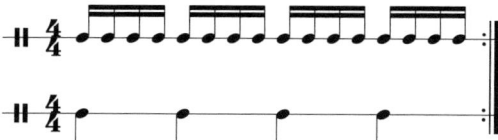 subdivision:

Now read through the following series of patterns, continuing to hear the above pattern as your internal guide. You'll notice that as you progress through the exercises, each subsequent first note is reduced by the length of one semiquaver (sixteenth note). Keep the subdivision going in your mind throughout:

So now of course you know a better answer to that question posed at the start of this section! If you understand basic subdivision, you simply *feel* the three quavers (eighth notes) that make up the ♩. and so will be able to play it completely accurately.

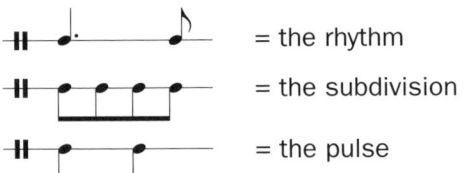

Layered subdivision

Here we come to a technique that will ultimately allow you to decode almost all rhythms.

Open the third element of the sight-reading web app, labelled *Rhythm*. The idea of this is to develop your ability to perceive these layers of subdivisions.

Set the tool up with the metronome at around 80bpm, and then click on ♩ (as the pulse) and add ♫ and ♬.

Click to start and spend some time listening to the three layers running simultaneously. Experiment by altering the volume of the layers (with the volume control). Turn down the pulse for example. Then turn it back up to full volume and turn down one of the other two subdivisions. Continue to experiment and listen carefully. Then turn the volume off for all layers and see if you can hear the sounds internally.

Here's another exercise, which I call *changing gear*. Begin by sensing the pulse, then gently change gear from one subdivision to the next. When you're more experienced, try mixing and matching two subdivisions simultaneously but at slightly different dynamic levels. The possibilities are endless. Try hearing the following example in your head, making up your own continuation.

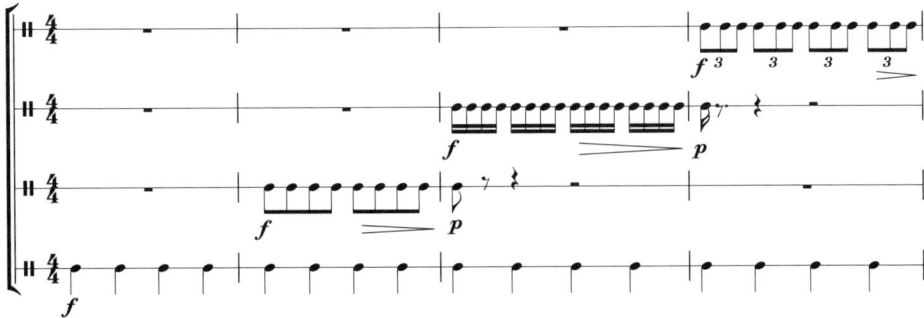

Ultimately the idea is to have this metronome with its layers of subdivision (virtually) accessible in your head as and when you need it! And because you understand it – and understand it so well – you will be able to manipulate it (internally), which will help decode just about any rhythmic pattern you might encounter. The layers of subdivision are, as it were, always there and you just increase or decrease the volume as necessary.

Once you feel comfortable with the basic ♩ ♫ ♬ layers, experiment with other note values and combinations (including compound time) using the sight-reading app.

> Select a piece or song you are currently teaching or learning; decide on the appropriate subdivisions necessary to decode all the rhythms and set these on the app. Then start the app and read the piece or song through carefully with the app sounding. In doing so, you should be aware that you know exactly how to realise the rhythmic shapes. Do this a few times with the app sounding, then switch off the app but continue to hear the layered subdivisions internally. This will ultimately become instinctive.

For example, this piece would best be decoded with a ♫ and ♬ subdivision:

Eventually you should be able to alter (internally) the volume of the appropriate subdivision (see above).

> Spend some time developing your inner metronome – it will reap inestimable benefits.

3.8 Location awareness and fingering

[30] For pianists, see also *Keyboard geography* on page 60.

To be fluent at sight-reading we need to know where the notes are on our instrument![30] If the brain needs additional time to process where a note is to be found (or consider the most appropriate fingering) then inevitably there will be an interruption to the flow, resulting in a hesitant moment, or simply unrhythmic playing or singing.

So it is important to know the names of the notes and to be able to find them on your instrument immediately. If there are known gaps here, spend some time systematically filling them in.

> Make sure, as a prerequisite, that you know (and *know* that you know!) the names of the notes on the stave related to the appropriate clef.
>
> - Lines in the treble 'E G B D F'
> - Spaces in the treble 'F A C E'
> - Lines in the bass 'G B D F A'
> - Spaces in the bass 'A C E G'
>
> In your mind's eye imagine each of these notes: 'seeing' the note on the stave and, simultaneously, *thinking* its letter name.

This can then be further developed in activities with or without actual notation.

Without notation:

Think of the name of a note

Picture its notation (in your mind's eye)

Play or sing it[31]

[31] Singers will need to play a note as a starting point and then think the pitch of the next note as related to that first pitch. It's all about intervals and relative pitch. Singing students will need a point of reference for pitch. If they don't already play an instrument or have a piano available, there are keyboard apps available that will help.

With notation:

> Read through what you are about to play and be sure you know the name of each note and where to find it without hesitation. If there are any uncertain notes make the connection strongly. Make a list of any such notes and redo the 'without notation' activity above.

Fingering

The point of fingering – the kind of 'helpful' fingering you might find marked in a piece – is usually to make sure that the hand (or fingers, or both hands) is in the right configuration (or place) to play the next note correctly and comfortably, with the added bonus of setting us up to move easily on to the *next* next note!

But let's look at fingering a little more closely. The concept has a slightly different meaning depending on what instrument you play.

Wind and brass

In studying these instruments as beginners, we learn the *fingering* of each new note – the kind of fingerings found in a fingering chart. What we learn is a finger combination that gives us, say, the note C. That's a *passive* fingering and as we progress it's useful to understand those fingerings as passive fingerings. The *active* fingering is what we have to do to get there from whatever the previous note is.

Strings

For string players (and guitarists), *passive* fingerings are less important. As players progress, the choice of fingering certain notes becomes greater as the player learns to move up and down the fingerboard with more understanding and control.

Pianists

For pianists, the concept of *passive* fingering doesn't apply. Here, in a sense, we have the most freedom because virtually any finger (or thumb) can play any note. Choosing wisely allows fluency.

The way to develop the skill of fingering on any instrument is through the careful practice of scales and all their related patterns. And again, work at these from written notation. Study the notation carefully as you play and think about what you do in order to get from one note to the next.

Here are three examples of the type of helpful fingerings you might find in an edited edition.

This example for clarinet will be helped by selecting the appropriate alternative fingerings to allow the phrase to be played *legato*:

These fingerings for violin will help guide the player to the best choices in order to be in the right place, minimise string crossing and play with a uniform sound (by avoiding open strings, for example):

This fingering for piano will help find the best next finger (or thumb) to allow the necessary movement of hand position, enabling the performance to move forward fluently:

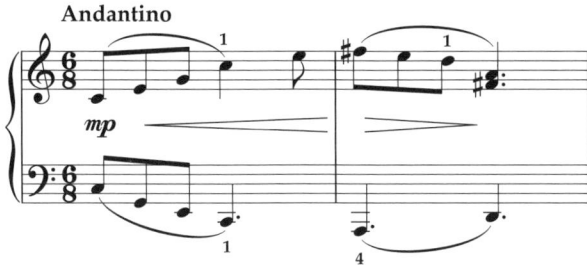

Learning scales and their associated patterns will help make these movements instinctive. If they have been practised thoroughly in scale work, then when you see these patterns occurring when sight-reading, you will instinctively know what to do. There will be no time lag for your brain to process any appropriate technical information.

3.9 Improvisation

Curiously, there are many links between sight-reading and improvisation – which, on first consideration, would seem to be two activities at different ends of the musical spectrum.

- Both are concerned with the unknown: in a sense you don't know what's coming next.
- Both are undertaken without (much) preparation.
- Both require the performer to adapt to the moment: rather like playing football or tennis, the next thing is not one that has been prepared beforehand.
- Both develop one's predictive skills: you develop the ability to have an idea of what might be coming next. What does come next might in some cases be predictable, while other times might be something of a surprise. But being aware of what it *might* be can be very useful.
- Both require a healthy dose of musical instinct.

Some musicians are quite intimidated by the thought of improvising. If you are, here's an exercise to change that view:

> Think of a piece you are currently learning and make a list of the ingredients – maybe those that are found in the first bar:
>
> - Key
> - Time signature
> - A rhythmic pattern
> - Dynamic level
> - Articulation
> - Character
>
> Using those very same ingredients make up just one bar of music. It's not intimidating at all! Then develop this idea – make up longer passages with the same ingredients. You'll soon be improvising with confidence.[32]

In the early stages of developing this kind of practical improvisation,[33] begin with a particular ingredient in mind – and then develop it in whichever ways seem musical and artistic.

[32] Try this link for a short video I've prepared on the way into improvisation: tinyurl.com/ImprovSR.

[33] I use the term 'practical improvisation' in the sense of using improvisation as a means of helping to develop understanding of an ingredient or combination of ingredients. Rather than improvisation being an intrinsic part of a style – like jazz or organists extemporising at a service.

> Here are some ingredients on which to base your short improvisations:
> - a key, using particular scale or arpeggio patterns
> - a particular rhythmic pattern which can be developed
> - a particular melodic shape or combination of shapes
> - a particular interval or combination of intervals – especially useful for singers
> - a harmonic progression like V – I or IV – I
> - a simple structure, like AB or ABA

Once you are confident, combine as many of the above as you feel able. As you become still *more* confident and feel able to improvise more freely and continuously, let your musical imagination roam and see what it suggests for what comes next.

Other predictions we can make

If you are improvising in say, G major, you might well make use of the closely related keys such as C and D major and E minor. The same is true when you are sight-reading in G major: it is a good idea to think of these keys before you begin. In time, making the connection with closely related keys should become instinctive. In other words, you will be prepared for patterns in these particular keys (you are predicting that they might appear) and so the process of reading them will be enhanced. This will also strengthen and add more substance to your ability to think in a key.

It's very useful to develop our predictive musical mind for sight-reading, in the sense that part of the brain is considering the likely next thing to happen. Whether the next thing is what we have predicted or not is not so important. It's simply yet another part of our musical thinking which, in broad terms, will make us even more musical and aware sight-readers.[34]

[34] This is not unlike playing chess. There is an interesting paper to be found in the Journal of Psycholinguistic Research (Vol 5, No 2, 1976) entitled *A Cognitive Model of Musical Sight-reading* by Thomas Wolf, in which many connections are made between sight-reading and chess!

Sight-reading technique – a summary

As you can see from the previous sections, we have identified nine areas of specific development that together will add up to *sight-reading technique*:

- Knowledge and understanding of ingredients
- Reading and hearing in our heads
- Brain processing speed and pattern recognition
- Peripheral vision and looking ahead
- 'Walking the course'
- Key awareness
- Subdivision
- Location awareness and fingering
- Improvisation

Like any technique, you should build it at a comfortable pace, and you will be aware of incremental improvement in each area. And like your instrumental or singing technique, do try to give it quality practice time on a regular basis. At least once or twice a week, though the best results will obviously materialise if you practise sight-reading every day, maybe choosing two or three areas to work on at each session.

3.10 Piano-specific techniques

Keyboard geography: knowing where the notes are

If you watch confident and experienced sight-readers (such as accompanists), you'll notice they don't look down at the keyboard very often. As a pianist, it's important to develop a very strong feel for where the notes are – in your mind. Gradually you should find that you reduce the necessity to look down at the keyboard. So – try all these activities *without* looking at the keyboard:

1. Find middle C. How did you do this? Maybe instinctively, but it's more helpful if we think about it in this way: you know that to the right of the note C there are two black notes and there is a white note to its left. Again, without looking at the keyboard, feel your way around this area of the instrument. Feel those black notes and the space to the left across to the B flat. Play these notes, again without looking directly at the keyboard. Now find all the other Cs.

2. Find an F. An F also has a white note to its left but the group of *three* black notes to its right, which ensures you're about to play an F rather than a C. Again, feel the shape of the patterns with your fingers, made by the location of the black and white notes in this particular area.

3. Find a D. Young pianists are often introduced to this note as the *dog in a kennel* (for obvious reasons!).

4. Find a D minor triad. Once the D is found this should offer no problems. Find other triads. Think the names of the notes you are playing.

5. Find a G♯, which of course is in the middle of the set of three black notes.

6. Find a note of your choice (no looking at the keyboard!) and then choose a different note to find and play. Begin within an octave span, but gradually make the distances greater.

7. Without looking at the keyboard, go straight to a random note and then work out what it is by feeling around it (those with perfect pitch needn't include this activity!). Repeat this often, trying to increase your processing speed.

8. Find and explore octaves in both hands.

9. Find and play arpeggios in all keys – 'think' the pitch names of the notes as you are playing them and imagine them written down or printed.

10. Explore jumps in the left hand, for example:

Try a different key each time you practise and vary the inversion of the chords. As you become more proficient and confident, make the jumps wider.

Enjoy and create more similar exercises for a few moments each time you practise, and gradually include more sophisticated ingredients.

As you do more reading be conscious of how much you look down at the keyboard and try to avoid doing so if possible – it takes up valuable time and you temporarily lose your place in the music.

Reading vertically as well as horizontally

We have dealt with the fact that the eye/brain process can only take in the details of one line of music at a time[35] and in a sense that's not something to be concerned about. Deciding on what exactly we look at next is not a *conscious* decision we make as we are sight-reading. The eyes are able to move very fast and if we are increasing our brain processing speed, then inputting and understanding all the necessary data will be happening automatically and quickly. Vertical and horizontal eye movements are being made naturally and continually with the reader building up a picture of what is there. Watch someone else's eye movements as they are sight-reading.

Multiple note patterns, chords and chord shapes

It's very useful to know such patterns, including chords and all the various versions in which they come. Here is a list of the more common examples. Imagine the shapes in your mind's eye and then play them, preferably without looking at the keyboard. Also find examples in printed music.

- Octaves
- Triads and their inversions, including augmented and diminished versions
- Four-note chords and their inversions
- Dominant and diminished 7th chords and their inversions

Knowledge of specific styles

Always be on the look-out for cadences and conventional and traditional pianistic patterns. If you recognise an *alberti* bass or a typical waltz left-hand figure for example, you can access the predictive feature of your sight-reading technique, which will help make the reading less pressurised and more fluent.

[35] See page 39.

4 Practical matters

It became clear through my sight-reading survey (see page 9) that teaching and learning sight-reading has not always been a happy experience. Having reached this point in this book I hope to have completely overturned any negative perception of the teaching, learning and practising of sight-reading you may have had. And also to have persuaded you that the 'just go and practise it and you will improve' type of approach is perhaps not the best.

But before we begin to look into the practical aspects of teaching and learning sight-reading, here are a number of interesting comments from the survey; both positive and negative. Each of them represents a particular scenario or approach we may relate to, or may have experienced in one way or another:

> *'I loved sight-reading and did it all the time so it was never an issue.'*
>
> *'I was forced to sight-read and hated it!'*
>
> *'I was curious as to how pieces sounded that I hadn't yet learnt. Curiosity which my teacher encouraged and so I learnt to enjoy sight-reading.'*
>
> *'I didn't enjoy learning it because I was terrible at it.'*
>
> *'I enjoyed being in an advanced choir as a child, and so became very good at reading.'*
>
> *'Actually, I was lazy with practising but just enjoyed sight-reading stuff, so got good at it.'*
>
> *'Some pieces are great to sight-read, especially if they're easy!'*
>
> *'I find it really frustrating and so prefer to miss it out of my practice.'*
>
> *'I'm really frightened of getting it wrong.'*

The following sections deal with practical ways to encourage sight-reading to become part of the regular learning regime. All negative thoughts, such as those above, will hopefully be entirely eliminated and this will encourage all, ultimately, to build an entirely positive attitude towards it.

4.1 Teaching and practising sight-reading

> Before we get going, maybe now is the moment to consider deeply, if you haven't already, your own attitude towards teaching and practising sight-reading. Be honest! If there *is* any negativity there, this will probably find its way into your teaching. You really need to be entirely convinced that it *can* be taught and learnt and that in so doing, your student's musical development will be much enhanced.

There are a number of sight-reading methods available, but if you'll forgive me, I'm going to explain how to use the *Improve Your Sight-reading!* [36] series here, though the approach in general will work for other sight-reading methods too. I've always been interested in the process of reading and one of the first 'reference' books I bought with my (quite modest) schoolboy pocket money was (slightly oddly for a 16-year-old), *Read Better, Read Faster* by Manya and Eric Leeuw.[37] I remember even then being very interested in the process and in fact one of my very first publications was *30 Miniature Duets for clarinets – a progressive guide to sight-reading*.

The *Improve Your Sight-reading!* series is very much underpinned by a basic understanding of the scientific processes involved and all the books are laid out in the same format. They are particularly useful in exam preparation, but more broadly offer a complete sequential and systematic course in learning to sight-read virtually from beginner right up to a really quite advanced level.

Let's have a look at how best to work through them from both the teaching and learning angle. But before we do, there is one rule I'd like you to consider carefully – and to try not to break!

[36] There are versions for most instruments and although they are 'graded' in the UK editions they provide a very good method for learning to sight-read from scratch, whether or not an exam is anywhere on the horizon!

[37] Penguin Books

> **Never sight-read anything that is not fully understood**

If we regularly attempt things we can't do (or even can't *quite* do) it gradually builds up a negative mindset that inevitably will not take us to a good place. Spending a little more time to guarantee understanding beforehand is an approach worth its weight in gold.

How best to use the *Improve Your Sight-reading!* series

Rhythmic exercises

Each stage in each book begins with Rhythmic Exercises (using the word rhythm in its 'succession of notes with particular values of duration' meaning). They consist of two lines of music: the lower line represents the pulse and the upper line a rhythm that relates to the pulse. It really is very important that these are properly understood before proceeding. Here's an example:

These exercises can be practised a number of ways and students should be encouraged to try all of them – maybe the most important is the first:

- Decide on a pulse and then hear both lines internally and simultaneously. The lower line perhaps as a thud, or a throb, or bass drum. It's that *sense of pulse* that we wish to develop as something we can always 'turn on' at whatever volume or intensity we need. The upper line can be 'heard' as a crisp side drum, the sound of our instrument, a car horn or cockerel or anything that might catch the imagination.
- The teacher taps (or a metronome sounds) the lower line while the student claps or taps the upper line.
- Tap the lower line with a foot and clap or tap the upper line.
- Tap one line with one hand and the other line with the other hand on a table-top or flat surface. Ideally repeat, reversing hands.
- Tap the lower line and sing or play the upper line on a note (or notes) of your choice.

Each time an exercise is attempted, begin by counting two bars in – one aloud and the second silently as a pulse. As students become more confident with this then just sensing the pulse for a bar is sufficient. But don't omit this essential activity.

If more than one Rhythmic Exercise is completed in a practice session, be sure to vary the tempo between exercises. We do get used to sight-reading pieces and exercises at the *same* tempo!

Developing your sense of layered subdivision

To develop accuracy further, students can also apply the technique of layered subdivision (see page 52). To do so, add a third line and hear the pulse and its subdivision (use a different 'sound' for this line):

The next line would be a ♫♫ subdivision (again use a different 'sound' for this line):

Once the concept of layered subdivision is really understood and your *sophisticated internal metronome* becomes accessible then, as you play, you should be **sensing the pulse, which is always apparent and secure, and a subdivision which can be increased or decreased in 'volume' or intensity as appropriate** (as shown in the example below). This will allow the rhythm to be realised with absolute accuracy. It may take a little time to develop this ability fully – but once it is installed, you'll *always* be able to decode rhythm.

From *Improve your sight-reading!* Grade 6, both staves of the Rhythmic Exercises have independent rhythms. The most straightforward way to do these exercises, having heard them internally, is to tap the pulse with a foot (or have it sounding on a metronome), then tap the upper line with the right hand and the lower line with the left (on a flat surface or knees perhaps). Ultimately the pulse and both lines can be heard completely internally.

> ### Rhythmic Exercises – a checklist
> - Decide on an appropriate pulse.
> - Sense the pulse.
> - Count in two bars: one aloud (or a whisper) and the second as a sense of pulse.
> - Try the exercises in different ways (as suggested above).

Melodic Exercises
The second stage in *Improve your sight-reading!* is Melodic Exercises. This example comes from the same stage as the Rhythmic Exercise above.

The rhythms used in these exercises are based on those learnt in the Rhythmic Exercises. First be sure the rhythm *is* absolutely understood. This is the time you need to know that you know! It's a very good idea to hear the rhythm internally first. Then check the technical side of things – fingerings, changes of hand position, shifting, alternative keywork and so on. Again, feel confident that nothing technical will impede the flow.

Then think through the following:

- Think about the key. Play the scale and arpeggio from notation and from memory (have a scale book handy whenever you're working on sight-reading). Think about your instrument *in that key!* Imagine the notes of the scale or the arpeggio metaphorically glowing on your instrument! Pianists can imagine the notes of the key in a different colour; other players can imagine the finger patterns, for example. In other words, turn on the 'thinking in a key' mechanism.

- Look for patterns – these may be rhythmical or melodic, based on scale or arpeggio shapes, repetitive, sequential, etc. Also look for repeated notes and rests – anything that allows you to *consciously* look ahead.

- Play the first note, decide on a pulse and then, hearing one bar of pulse as an introduction, try to hear the piece internally – melody and rhythm. The pitch accuracy may be variable but you will improve.[38]

[38] Singers have to produce their own pitch so quite a bit of the learning time (in lessons and practice) will be devoted to pitching intervals confidently and accurately. So when singers hear internally there is more necessity to aim for the correct pitch straight away.

The Melodic Exercises, up to and including Grade 5 (in all the books) have no additional markings (such as dynamics and articulation – except for slurs). This is to allow full concentration on processing rhythm and melodic shapes.

Working methodically through all the Melodic Exercises in all the books is rather like building up a musical vocabulary. You will meet and come to recognise melodic patterns that recur again and again, just as they do with words and phrases when reading text.

Melodic Exercises – a checklist

- Check for anything that might require some particular technical control.
- Decide on an appropriate pulse.
- Hear the music in your head.
- Think about looking ahead – are there any patterns?
- Begin when you're certain you really understand it.
- Count in two bars: one aloud and the second as a sense of pulse.

Prepared pieces

The Prepared Pieces that follow come with some questions which are designed to help you begin thinking about and processing the pieces practically and musically.

Again, the following comes from the same stage as both examples above:

1. This piece begins on an up-beat. What does this mean?
2. On your knees or a flat surface, tap the pulse with one hand and the rhythm with the other.
3. Are there any repeated rhythmic patterns?
4. Imagine all the notes affected by the key signature as being coloured red.
5. Play the first note and hear the piece in your head before playing it.

First of all, look through the piece and decide on a tempo and thus a pulse. Then work through the questions carefully. Use the 'walking the course' technique in addition to the questions, particularly making sure that all ingredients are noticed. For example: melodic shapes; ascending and descending patterns; rhythmic patterns, phrase shapes, fingering, hand positions, musical details and anything else that will help to define the piece's particular identity. The intention is to develop the feeling that *the music is completely understood*. Read through the piece silently. Begin when it is fairly certain that it will be played accurately and fluently! Remember to set the pulse going first. And because the ingredients are understood, there should be plenty of brain space for the musical and expressive details too.

Once played, evaluate the performance – observationally and objectively. With the careful preparation undertaken there should have been no errors or hesitation. If there were, think what might have caused them and then have another go.

Improvise and compose
Some of the books also contain short improvisation and composition exercises. The usefulness of improvisation is explained on page 57. Composing short tunes using relevant ingredients is also very worthwhile. Try to compose your piece in your head and then write it down. And it's fun then reading and playing or singing your own tunes.

Going Solo
At the end of each Stage we come to a number of examples that put everything learned so far into a series of short pieces to practise reading at sight. You rarely ever have to read with *absolutely* no sight of the music beforehand. In most exams, for example, you are given maybe half a minute to look through the music first. So, spend around 30 seconds *reading* the music carefully, discovering, absorbing and processing as much information as possible. Feel that after this short but intense investigation, to some considerable extent you really understand the music and know what it means. There should be little to faze you: rhythm, knowing and thinking in the key, recognising

patterns of all types, technical control and musical meaning should all be entirely within your understanding and control.

Then play the piece. If the general preparation was all-inclusive then the experience of playing will have been confident and pleasurable. You will have known you were in control. You will have known you were getting it right as you were playing it. There would have been sufficient brain space available to be aware of what you were doing as you were doing it.

If there was a slip along the way, you can think about it positively afterwards and objectively work out why. Hopefully the next time a similar situation occurs you will have even more awareness and control.

How much of a lesson should be devoted to sight-reading?

An interesting question that can be considered in a number of ways. In a sense, because everything is connected, much of any lesson is devoted, by default, (if sometimes indirectly) to sight-reading.

In my survey, about 75% of teachers suggested that they spend about five minutes or less of an average lesson on sight-reading. (A small number did no sight-reading work at all.) About 15% do more than five minutes and about 10% leave it to pupils to do at home.

What is important is that, in each lesson, we incorporate as many of the essential sight-reading skills as possible. And in doing so, be confident in the knowledge that these are transferable and will impact on a student's general musical development. For example, always 'thinking' a pulse before beginning to play or sing; developing the concept of layered subdivision; noticing and understanding rhythmic and melodic patterns; understanding the concept of thinking in a key, really *reading* the music and much more. If we are teaching using the Simultaneous Learning approach, this will be happening automatically. In this way, though not directly working at sight-reading, you will be nevertheless constantly developing it indirectly as part of a student's overall musical growth.

How much practice time should be devoted to sight-reading?

Obviously, there is no definitive answer to this! If a student is really thinking about what they are doing, which would include considering theory aspects, consciously internally hearing what they are reading (whether it's at sight or not), thinking in subdivisions as necessary, and maybe doing some improvisation, then they should be indirectly improving their broader sight-reading skills.

And if students understand the importance of being a good reader, and really understand *how* to work at all the various aspects discussed in this book, then they should enjoy spending time specifically on the subject anyway. Ideally students will get used to doing, for example, a page or two from the relevant *Improve Your Sight-reading!* book at each practice. This would typically take just a few minutes. And once we begin enjoying a task and can sense progress, we become more motivated and may do even more!

Some teachers think that if their students find appropriate music and read it regularly, they will improve their sight-reading. Unless this is very well managed (and students have a substantial library of appropriate music to choose from *and* have good judgement in choosing it) it is a strategy sadly destined to fail (except in rare cases) and may end up in causing serious sight-reading phobia! Here is an interesting and relevant response from my survey:

> 'My teacher told me just to read anything I could find, which I did for a while. But it was always too difficult so eventually I gave up and sight-reading always felt uncomfortable.'

In the earlier stages of learning we often move on a little too quickly – the next piece always a little more demanding than the previous. When learning to read, schools have shelves of books at the same level and the children are encouraged to read as many as they can. Providing lots of material at a *similar level* is very important when learning to read music, too.[39] And as long as this is managed carefully, reading new material should become a pleasure.

[39] This is the idea behind my series *A Piece a Week* (Faber Music).

4.2 Sight-reading in exams

> 'You've got an exam coming up – I guess we'd better do some work on sight-reading…'

This is a scenario we've all probably encountered at some point or another. If we are teaching in the manner described in this book, this situation should not arise. Students will understand notation and the sight-reading element of an exam should become one that is keenly anticipated, with students *knowing* that they will be able to read and play or sing whatever comes along.

In the weeks before an exam it may be an idea to begin preparing appropriate pieces in a particular way, in order to make the exam experience totally familiar and secure.

Below is a series of activities in the Simultaneous Learning style that will instil a disciplined, thorough, enjoyable and entirely confident approach to the sight-reading element of an exam. And the process is virtually the same whether it's the first or the final grade level that you're preparing for.

If you and your student have been working systematically through all the techniques and activities in this book, the sight-reading element of an exam should hold no fears at all. But you might like to focus your work as the exam approaches. There are two journeys outlined below. The first is more comprehensive and might be undertaken (as many times as you wish) from about a month before the exam for about two weeks and the second will then take you right up to the exam.

So let's go on these two journeys, which will ultimately arrive at real sight-reading confidence. They set out appropriate logical and sequential activities and make appropriate connections from the *Simultaneous Learning Musical Map of the World*.

Journey 1 – taken about a month prior to the exam

Repeat this as often as you can, each time with an appropriate exam-style practice piece.[40] You don't need to follow the sequence below too strictly – it's a flavour of what you might do. See what feels right for you or your student. Miss out any activities you don't feel you need to have a go at.

So, with the piece you are preparing to sight-read:

---

[40] There are many appropriate pieces in the *Improve Your Sight-reading!* books or you can use specimen sight-reading pieces published by exam boards.

[41] Pianists can follow the main musical ideas in a piece in order to clap a continuous rhythm. Or just choose the right- or left-hand line.

Step	Category
Decide on an appropriate pulse	Rhythm
Hear the pulse internally and switch on your internal layered subdivision metronome as necessary	Aural
Count the pulse aloud, read and clap the rhythm,[41] noticing any repeated patterns	Rhythm
Hearing the pulse internally, read and clap the rhythm then clap the pulse and read and hear the rhythm internally	Rhythm/Aural
Choose all or part of the piece and improvise using the rhythm and appropriate notes	Improvisation
Play the scale and arpeggio of the key and switch on your 'thinking in the key' mechanism	Key
Improvise in the key using rhythms from the piece	Improvisation
Look for any repeated melodic patterns.	Theory
Read the music, hearing the pitch and rhythm internally	Aural
Hear, internally and *from memory*, as much as you can	Aural/memory
Notice and think about dynamic markings and articulation markings	Theory
Consider the character and how you will convey it	Character
Reading the music, hear the whole piece internally with all the ingredients included	Aural
Are there any fingerings or technical matters to consider?	Technique
Set the pulse going again and with your internal layered sub-division metronome available if you need it, perform the piece	Performance

Then evaluate the performance. If all was set up well, your student should have felt: 'I know (more or less) exactly what this piece is about and know (more or less) that I will play it correctly.' If that wasn't the case then spend more time on the preparation. Remember the rule introduced earlier: *never sight-read anything that isn't fully understood* – it just wastes time!

If there was a small slip along the way, you'll probably know why – and so it doesn't really matter. Play it again if you'd like to iron it out.

I'm occasionally asked, having carried out this activity, if the final performance was indeed 'sight-reading' given all the preparation. My answer is *yes*. The performance is still the first time the piece was read and played. And it's very rare that we ever have to read and play anything *literally* without any prior sight or preparation (even if the preparation time is very short).

Journey 2

Moving on to *Journey 2* about two weeks before the exam, we begin to set up the exam-style scenario:

Step	Focus
Decide on an appropriate pulse and hear it internally	Rhythm/aural
Run your eyes over the rhythm – there should be nothing you won't understand	Rhythm
Identify the key and switch on your 'thinking in key' mechanism	Key
Notice any repeated patterns – rhythm or melodic – and any dynamic and articulation markings	Theory
Consider the character and how you will convey it	Character
Read (internally) the whole piece with all the ingredients included	Aural
Are there any fingerings or technical matters to consider?	Technique
Set the pulse going again and with your internal layered sub-division metronome available if you need it, perform the piece	Performance

As this routine becomes familiar, you'll find it takes less and less time to complete. You'll probably find that you can do certain activities simultaneously and some you may miss out as they become instinctive or automatic. Half a minute will eventually feel very generous for running through the whole process, and the exam experience will be one of self-assured pleasure rather than panic-ridden stress.

Playing musically when sight-reading in exams…

…is of course no different from playing musically at any other time! And all the usual considerations apply. But, with the various ingredients now understood and in control there should be brain space available for making the performance musical, too. Look at the markings: the tempo and any additional qualification; a title if there is one and dynamic markings. Then make some quick decisions on tempo and approach (a rich warm *legato* or a light articulation, for example). Include lots of dynamic variation if you can. Examiners like dynamics! In a sense these fall into three types:

Marked dynamics: make good contrasts if there are only a small number actually marked in the music.

Directional dynamics: a feeling of *crescendo,* for example, to help an energetic piece move forwards (but not too much!).

Expressive dynamics: those extra *crescendi* and *diminuendi* used (sometimes marked but more often added by the performer) to shape a phrase or melody.

The ingredients in the sight-reading element of an exam are almost always much simpler than those found in the pieces played. Logically speaking then, sight-reading in exams really should hold no fear! Preparing carefully in the manner set out in this book and particularly in this section should result in exam candidates positively looking forward to their sight-reading!

4.3 The first encounter with notation

If we get this right, we can set our student up for life as a confident sight-reader. Before we embark on our very first reading then playing/singing experience, do ensure the basics are strongly in place:

Make sure...
- ...that any necessary technical control is secure: hand shape and position, breathing or bowing, for example.
- ...the names of the notes are known (also securely!).
- ...you have introduced the sense of pulse (see page 27) and that it is also understood.

At some point in the lesson (before working on the actual reading and playing from the notation) get your pupil to read a few words silently. Ask them about the experience. Try to draw out two points:

- that they would have heard the sound of the words in their head
- and that they would have understood the meaning of those words.

Try the following sequence of logical Simultaneous Learning-style activities.

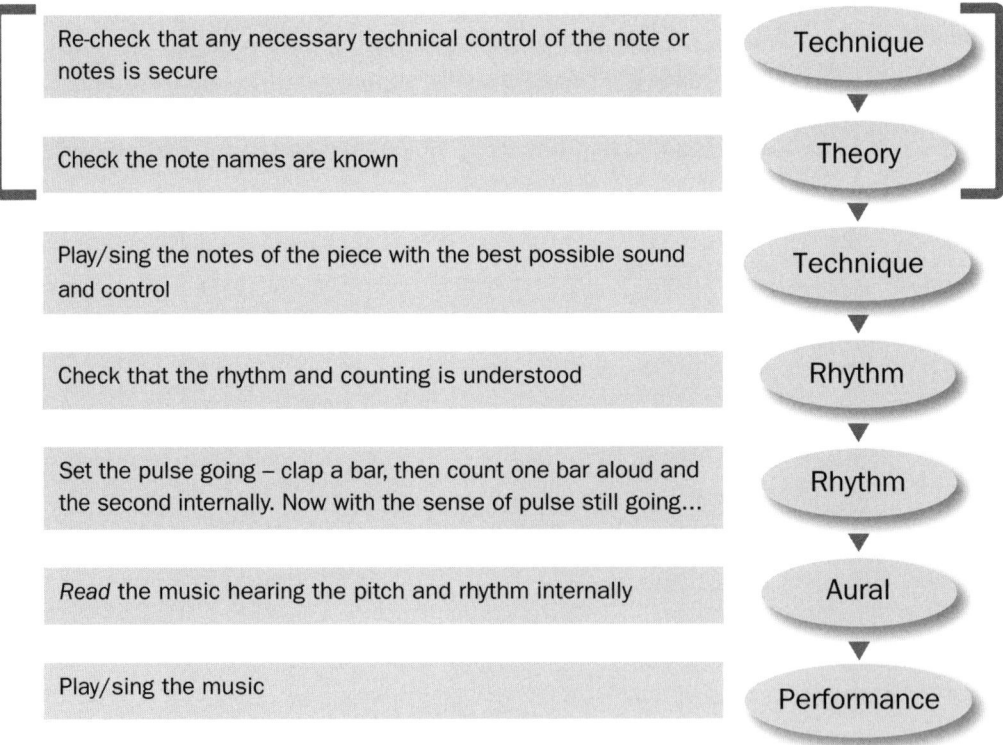

The first two activities may be unnecessary:
Before actually playing or singing, your pupil should completely understand the notation, knowing both how to bring it to life technically and what it will sound like. They were truly *reading* the music – sight-reading in fact, with complete control and no stress.

With this kind of preparation on a *regular basis*, you can see how a student will truly learn to read music – and that sight-reading will hold no fears for them.

4.4 FAQs

> 'My pupils always think sight-reading is too difficult. Often because they tend to play too quickly and refuse to believe that slower is better. How can I stop them rushing?'

Many students, when you suggest that they might like to practise *slowly*, equate slow with boring! What we generally mean by slow practice is slowing the pulse, thus lengthening the time it takes to get to the next note or beat – or the next 'event'. The problem for many is that they don't fill that extra time with anything useful and so slowly get bored.

In *slow-motion practice* the idea is that you fill that time by processing what you will actually do to bring the next 'event' to life – being aware of thinking the subdivisions carefully, which fingers you will move, some specific bow control or breathing, managing a change of dynamic, an intensifying of the character – or whatever is appropriate. It makes the practice very efficient. In a sense, you are actually programming your brain to carry out the appropriate sequence of events. So at a faster speed, which is really allowing the next event to be sooner, the control is becoming automatic. The label *slow-motion practice* makes it much more approachable.

This is a particularly appropriate way to practise sight-reading – and always ensure students sight-read at the right speed *for them*.

> 'I often lose my place when I'm sight-reading in ensembles. What should I do?'

When taking part in a rehearsal, players occasionally lose their place. If you have practised reading music using the method discussed in this book, this will not be a problem. You will be able to find your place again, because you are aware of the ingredients and will be able to follow the music without having to stop the rehearsal.

If someone was reading this book to you aloud (from their copy) and you were following along in your copy and you were distracted for a moment or two, you would soon find your place again. You would recognise the words they were saying and match them to the words you had in front of you.

The technique is much the same in a musical situation. You would be hearing what's going on around you and therefore be able to use the clues to pinpoint where you should be in your own part. If your internal metronome system is active that will strongly assist in knowing where you are in terms of bar structure.

Also, the more confident orchestral players become as sight-readers the more they will be able to pay attention to the conductor – they will be able to get their eyes off the music more often as the memory develops.

> 'I'd like a regular activity for the end of lessons that makes sight-reading fun for my students. What can you suggest?'

Playing or singing duets (from notation) has long been a lesson activity enjoyed by both teacher and students. There are many good reasons for including this regularly. Maybe the most central point is learning the importance of keeping going and thus ignoring small slips if they are made. Ideally players will use a small part of their brain space to acknowledge the slip but have the confidence to know where they are and simply carry on. Of course, it's very important to choose the music carefully avoiding anything that might include technical problems that could create hesitancy or any breakdown in fluency. Try to find interesting pieces that have a lot of character and musical markings. Do a little preparation in advance – maybe a brief 'walking the course' and then encourage the inclusion of lots of musical colour during the read through. Learners especially enjoy duets in which the teacher's part is more complex and the resultant performance sounds particularly impressive.

> 'Several of my students have dyslexia – can I improve their sight-reading technique?'

Experts in the field have written extensively about the issues that those with dyslexia face when reading both words and music. Those issues, which include visual tracking, decoding symbols, storing information in the working memory and physical coordination, can vary considerably from one individual to another, but there is general agreement that many with dyslexia can get a lot out of studying and indeed reading music and *are* able to make much progress. Many of the ideas presented in this book can be adapted with a positive expectation. And there is a lot to be learned from multisensory teaching techniques. One of the best resources available at the time of writing is the British Dyslexia Association's website.[42] There is a comprehensive section there on music, which includes an in-depth subsection on sight-reading.

[42] bdadyslexia.org.uk/advice/adults/music-and-dyslexia-1

Final thought

Sight-reading then is a technique that, through systematic teaching and learning, can be acquired by all who would like to develop it. And in so doing, the skill will take us to a clearly recognisable and very powerful place:

> **A confident and proficient sight-reader is a confident and proficient musician.**

As we have seen, the skill of sight-reading is an amalgam of virtually all aspects of being a musician. It combines and requires understanding of each of the three main areas of practical music making – technique, artistry and language. And it requires understanding and control in all the subsets of those areas.

Sight-reading is far from being an optional extra, an ability that's good to have but doesn't really matter if you don't have it. In fact it's one of the most central and important skills for all musicians to master and, if it is approached in the kind of methodical way as suggested in this book, there's nothing to stop anyone from doing so. Not only will you discover that this very important skill is not so challenging to acquire, but also that it will cause a significant improvement in all other aspects of your musical development too. And the more of us who can do it, the more chance this great art has of survival.

Also by Paul Harris

Improve your sight-reading!
This series of workbooks is designed to help overcome sight-reading problems, especially in the context of graded examinations. Step by step players build up a complete picture of each piece, first through rhythmic and melodic exercises, then by the study of prepared pieces with associated questions for the student to answer, and finally to a series of practice tests.

Unconditional Teaching
This inspirational new approach encourages teachers to explore and transform how they teach. By identifying and reimagining the barriers or 'conditions' that can stand in the way of effective teaching, it allows for the most immersive and positive learning experience. Ideas are tackled from both a practical and psychological perspective, rooted in Paul's renowned *Simultaneous Learning* methodology. This seminal book will begin your journey towards an unbounded, unconditional way of teaching.

The Virtuoso Teacher
By considering the 'virtuoso teacher' and how a teacher might attain virtuoso status, Paul Harris delves into the core issues of being a teacher and the teaching process. This seminal book takes a fascinating look at topics such as self-awareness and the importance of emotional intelligence; getting the best out of pupils; dealing with challenging pupils; asking the right questions; creating a masterplan; taking the stress out of learning and teaching for the right reasons.

The Practice Process
The Practice Process explores the key role the teacher plays in developing a psychological and holistic approach for pupils. Packed with clear advice, innovative ideas and principles, this book is firmly rooted in the *Simultaneous Learning* approach.